THE PENGUIN POETS

ROBERT FROST

Born in San Francisco in 1874, Robert Frost was brought to New England when he was 10, at his father's death. He went to Dartmouth College, married, studied at Harvard and between 1900 and 1905 farmed in New Hampshire and worked in mills in Lowell, Massachusetts, and as editor and teacher. But although his first published poem appeared when he was 19 ('My Butterfly'), only 14 poems were printed before 1918, and *A Boy's Will*, his first book, was published in England when he was 39. He had sold his farm, gone to London and cultivated the friendship of Edward Thomas. After three years and *North of Boston* (1914), he returned to America well known and settled in New Hampshire again. *New Hampshire* (1923) shows one of his few developments – towards politics and satire. *A Further Range* (1936) is more philosophically theoretical than earlier work, while the two *Masques* (1945, 1947) mark a third stage – concern with man's relations with God and ultimate metaphysical conditions. Frost by now had a wide public and numerous prizes and university posts and degrees, and was on the way to becoming America's unofficial laureate, tacitly acknowledged by his trips to Russia and Israel, and the invitation to read 'The Gift Outright' (1942) at President Kennedy's inauguration. Robert Frost died in 1963.

ROBERT FROST: SELECTED POEMS

Edited with an Introduction
by Ian Hamilton

PENGUIN BOOKS

Penguin Books Ltd, Harmondsworth, Middlesex, England
Penguin Books, 625 Madison Avenue, New York, New York 10022, U.S.A.
Penguin Books Australia Ltd, Ringwood, Victoria, Australia
Penguin Books Canada Ltd, 41 Steelcase Road West, Markham, Ontario, Canada
Penguin Books (N.Z.) Ltd, 182–190 Wairau Road, Auckland 10, New Zealand

—

The edition from which this selection is taken first
published in Great Britain as *The Poetry of Robert Frost*
by Jonathan Cape Ltd 1971
This selection from *The Poetry of Robert Frost*
published in Penguin Books 1973
Reprinted 1975, 1976

—

—

Made and printed in Great Britain by
Hazell Watson & Viney Ltd, Aylesbury, Bucks
Set in Monotype Bembo

CONTENTS

From WEST-RUNNING BROOK (1928)

From A FURTHER RANGE (1936)

From A WITNESS TREE (1942)

INTRODUCTION

Perhaps the chief difficulty in talking about Robert Frost, both for those who talked about him in his lifetime and for those who talk about him now, is the difficulty of separating the poetry from the public personality. During his lifetime Frost was the nearest thing to a 'national' poet that America possessed. His virtues and his wisdom were applauded as representatively, and hearteningly, Yankee – distilled from the soil, his poems spoke of rural labour, of dignified self-reliance, of shrewd, practical and yet respectful dealings with a nature he both loved and hated. They were also, much of the time, unblushingly conservative and patriotic. And better still, they seemed to *talk*; talk in a natural no-nonsense way – a more or less ordinary man talking to more or less ordinary men. Throughout his life, Frost assiduously cultivated this portrayal of himself as the lovable, plain-dealing New England farmer-poet. In hundreds of personal appearances, interviews and poetry readings, he did nothing to disappoint expectations of this sort. Here, for example, are two press cuttings he might well have enjoyed poring over:

> Robert Frost is a poet whose work and personal appearances have moved thousands of Americans to a demonstrativeness that might easily be associated with the presence of a heroic athlete or movie star. When he says his poems . . . it is to standing room only audiences. And the response is based not on superficial idolatry but on a deep set and affectionate admiration often bordering on awe . . . the impact of Robert Frost on poetry and those who love poetry is possibly less than his impact as a personality on anyone who gets near him . . . he is like no statesman, celebrity or ordinary human being . . . Robert Frost is quietly but unmistakably overwhelming.

This was written when Frost was eighty-four, four years before President Kennedy sent him to visit Russia as an ambassador of

Yankee straightforwardness. Over forty years earlier, though, Frost's personality was being praised in much the same drowsily ecstatic terms:

Mr Frost has windblown cheeks and clear blue eyes. Yankee of Yankees and glad of it ... Fresh from his farm on Sugar Hill, Franconia, New Hampshire, where Mt Lafayette towers and the Old Man of the Mountains frowns, Mr Frost is paying his first visit to Philadelphia. Quite recently he's been ski-ing over rugged country, tapping maple trees, and shaping up new poems.

And this for the whole of his career was the way America liked to see Frost and the way Frost wanted to be seen. It was a faultlessly sustained performance.

Needless to say, it was not a performance that everyone enjoyed; there were quite a few dissenting voices, particularly from fellow poets, and not all of them motivated by pure envy. The feeling was that far from doing poetry a service by peddling his rustic charm and by bowing to the patriotic plaudits, Frost was in fact selling poetry disastrously short. Here is a typical expression of that view – by Malcolm Cowley, writing in 1944:

We have lately been watching the growth in this country of a narrow nationalism that has spread from politics into literature (although its literary adherents are usually not political isolationists). They demand, however, that American literature should be affirmative, optimistic, uncritical and 'truly of this nation'. They have been looking round for a poet to exalt: and Frost, through no fault of his own (but chiefly through the weaker qualities of his work) has been adopted as their symbol. Some of the honours heaped upon him are less poetic than political. He is being praised too often and with too great vehemence by people who don't like poetry. And the result is that his honours shed very little of their luster on other poets, who in turn feel none of the pride in his achievement that a battalion feels, for example, when one of its officers is cited for outstanding services. Instead, Frost is depicted by his admirers as a sort of Sunday school paragon, a saint among miserable sinners. His common sense and strict Americanism are used as an excuse for berating and belittling other poets, who have supposedly fallen into the sins of pessimism, obscurity, obscenity and yielding to foreign influences...

These two ways of viewing Frost remained fairly constantly in evidence throughout his career – on the one hand, the popular idol, on the other the object of suspicion and some bitterness in the eyes of the highbrow-radical literary world, a world dominated during the period in which Cowley was writing by the ideals of complexity and abstruse wit inherited from T. S. Eliot and encouraged by the New Criticism. Frost, the New Critics could see, was more of a modernist than his popular reputation would allow him to admit, and they resented him for getting, finally, the best of both worlds.

Since Frost's death in 1963, there has been no effective alteration in this balance of opinion – not, at any rate, until two years ago when the second volume of the Frost biography appeared. The author, Lawrance Thompson, was Frost's own appointee, the 'official' choice to write the definitive life, and he had spent many years in Frost's company, apparently as a close friend, during the latter stages of the poet's life. The biography, however, when it appeared – and there is still a third volume to come – turned out to be not the pious tribute that might have been expected, but an elaborate and apparently vindictive essay in character-assassination. Frost emerged from Thompson's pages as anything but the sunny and lovable New England sage of popular legend. On the contrary he was presented as vain, morose, hypocritical and treacherous; as an opportunistic careerist who was prepared to lie, cheat and wound in order to win yet another crumb of adulation. When Frost had a new book coming out, we are told, he deliberately set out to ingratiate himself with prospective reviewers and influential editors; when prizes were in the offing he would make sure that he was on good terms with the jury; when a rival poet seemed to be making ground, he would attempt to impede his progress by a campaign of furtive vilification; when he scented the imminent power of a possibly hostile critic, he would neutralize the threat by making friends with him. All this, of course, went on in private;

in the foreground Frost was busily maintaining his air of innocence.

Although one comes away from Thompson's book disliking Thompson rather more than one dislikes Frost, it is none the less a damaging indictment. It is too early to say what the effects of it will be on Frost's popular standing in America but one thing is immediately clear; it will never again be possible for him to be viewed in quite the old way. And this, it seems to me, is all to the good – if Frost's popular following does fall away, as in large part it surely must, this will remove a major obstacle from the path of his genuine, and informed, admirers. It will also make it possible for the poetry to be got at in a new, uncluttered way, much more directly and sympathetically.

And if that happens, then one obvious point about the poetry will emerge more clearly than it has hitherto been able to. It will be seen, in other words, that however devious and self-promoting Frost was in his life, there *never was*, at bottom, anything very lovable about the appearance he makes in his own poems. Even his supposed virtues, the virtues that have been so widely thought to be endearing, are really much more negative than positive. They each have their harsh, misanthropic centre; they are almost always less to do with giving than with taking away. Lionel Trilling once caused a minor scandal by turning a speech of tribute to Frost's eighty-fifth birthday into an examination of what he called the 'terrifying' quality of the best of Frost's work, the utterly uncomforting and resolute sense of futility that much of it bears. He was thought to have behaved disgracefully, insulting the dear old man like that, and of course there has been a long, unthinking conspiracy among Frost's admirers to shut away what even they must have seen to be the essential desperation of much of even his most amiable work.

But before taking a look at what Frost's emotional universe centred on, it is important that one takes into account the stratagems employed by the poet to, as it were, negate his own negations. It is important, that is, to ask what his poetic, as distinct from his personal, charm amounted to. A lot of this charm, it will be readily agreed, has to do with Frost's famous speaking voice. The effort for a truly natural speech, a language of common men, is of course an ancient and rarely successful one. Frost was more successful than most; and at a less propitious time than that enjoyed by earlier contenders. Most of Frost's colloquial rhythms came to him intuitively during the long years of obscurity and neglect that preceded his discovery in England (Frost was in his forties before he won any real reputation as a poet), but his first book, *A Boy's Will*, is full of stiff, literary artificialities – the effort is *for* colloquialism, but at this stage he clearly didn't know how to mould either vocabulary or metre to his purposes. His contact with the English scene at a time when the whole of traditional poetic practice was being called in question – principally by the Imagists but also, in their more cautious way, by the Georgian group which Frost was most involved with – this contact could only have encouraged and focused his ambition for a relaxed naturalness of delivery. What is crucial, though, is that Frost took neither of the obvious or fashionable paths towards this naturalness – neither the path of free verse (for him, he once said, writing free verse would be like playing tennis with the net down) nor the other path of simply dropping in extra syllables here and there or removing them here and there, in order to oil the works of a basically mechanical traditionalism. The challenge he set himself was to risk admitting into a traditional framework what one might call the superfluities of talk – the hesitations, qualifications, repetitions, false starts, parentheses, and so on. His aim was to admit these whilst at the same time maintaining the regularized dignity of metrical speech. He put it this way:

> The living part of a poem is the intonation entangled somehow in the syntax, idiom and meaning of a sentence. It is only there for those who have heard it previously in conversation. It is not for us in any Greek or Latin poem because our ears have not been filled with the tones of Greek and Roman talk. It is the most volatile and at the same time important part of poetry. It goes and the language

becomes a dead language and the poetry dead poetry. With it go the accents, the stresses, the delays that are not the property of vowels and syllables but that are shifted at will with the sense. Vowels have length, there is no denying. But the accent of sense supersedes all other accents, overrides and sweeps it away.

There is no question but that much of Frost's charm derives from, quite simply, his over-exploitation of this procedure. It's often as if, having learned to talk naturally, he couldn't stop talking. Some of his long narratives and dialogues are precisely as prolix and tediously self-indulgent as real speech tends to be. But the spectacle of a man jawing on, as if at his own fireside of a winter's evening, and pretending to no degree of intellectualization or compression or literary artifice – this, and Frost certainly didn't spare himself in his efforts for such cosiness, was irresistible:

> He fell at Gettysburg or Fredericksburg.
> I ought to know – it makes a difference which:
> Fredericksburg isn't Gettysburg, of course.
> But what I'm getting to is how forsaken
> A little cottage this has always seemed . . .

The message seems to be that you can always trust a man who lets you catch him thinking aloud. There are of course huge tracts of Frost's work as irritatingly and wastefully 'colloquial' as this, and they become all the more irritating as, in his late poems, he begins dealing in craggy wisdom. But one can see, and respond to, the appeal. And one can see also that Frost needed this prolixity, this confidence in his freedom to ramble on, in order to achieve the triumphs of concentrated and subtle naturalness that one finds in the best of his shorter poems. 'Birches' is a famous example. Here Frost achieves the extraordinarily difficult task of both mounting the scene, pictorializing it in vivid and exact detail, and at the same time convincing us that he is – *at this moment* – pursuing a complex and precarious course of feeling, a course of feeling which we can observe shifting and developing as the local drama unfolds. What sustains the tension is the poem's achieved state of presentness, and this is made convincing by the authenticity of Frost's spoken rhythms:

So was I once myself a swinger of birches.
And so I dream of going back to be.
It's when I'm weary of considerations,
And life is too much like a pathless wood
Where your face burns and tickles with the cobwebs
Broken across it, and one eye is weeping
From a twig's having lashed across it open.
I'd like to get away from earth awhile
And then come back to it and begin over.
May no fate willfully misunderstand me
And half grant what I wish and snatch me away
Not to return. Earth's the right place for love:
I don't know where it's likely to go better.
I'd like to go by climbing a birch tree,
And climb black branches up a snow-white trunk
Toward heaven, till the tree could bear no more,
But dipped its top and set me down again.
That would be good both going and coming back.
One could do worse than be a swinger of birches.

In these, the poem's concluding lines, one notices in particular the finely calculated balancing of the elevatedly poetic with the low-colloquial. The flatness of 'And then come back to it and begin over' is subtly redeemed by the loftiness of 'May no fate willfully misunderstand me'. One notices also – and this crops up time and again in Frost's work – his ability to hit on natural or familiar turns of phrase which are in fact regular iambic pentameter – in these lines he is able to use his strict iambics to keep a check on the looser lines, but such is his knack that the iambic lines tend to be among the most natural, the most loose-sounding, in the poem – 'And so I dream of going back to be', 'I'd like to get away from earth awhile', 'And life is too much like a pathless wood', and so on.

The best-known lines in 'Birches': 'One could do worse than be a swinger of birches', 'Earth's the right place for love: I don't know where it's likely to go better', usefully illustrate another important ingredient of Frost's charm – his use of the aphorism, and in particular the aphorism that speaks of a resigned cheerfulness, or a cheerful resignation. Frost is a master of the stoic shrug, the rugged settling for what there is, however less than perfect. Behind this resignation there are in fact deep areas of fear and despair, but only intermittently are these allowed to show through. Frost uses his social manner, his maintaining of a brave face, as a defence against the real meanings (should one choose to follow those meanings right through) of many of his more popular, calendar-bound, aphorisms. Of course, as with his colloquial habit, the habit of nuggety wisdom was a seductive one and Frost was encouraged to indulge it. There is a determined eagerness to charm in lines like:

> The melancholy of having to count souls
> Where they grow fewer and fewer every year
> Is extreme when they shrink to none at all.
> It must be I want life to go on living.

or:

> If one by one we counted people out
> For the least sin, it wouldn't take us long
> To get so we had no one left to live with.
> For to be social is to be forgiving.

The point in each of these cases is excruciatingly banal and cheaply consolatory. At a more sophisticated level, though, one has a poem like 'The Road Not Taken' – a poem much-celebrated but one which seems to me to make a pretence of doing the bold things it says it's doing; a poem which is ultimately more concerned to be winning than disturbing. The poem's charm is in *seeming* to have engaged with a huge and central problem, the problem of moral choice. But the issues we are presented with are so vague and arbitrary that we are allowed to luxuriate in the delusion that we have actually been made to ponder them. The air of lostness, of irretrievable error that hangs over the poem is a beguiling means of disguising its essentially inert bleakness. To Frost, it doesn't seem to matter much which road he took, or didn't take. It is that indifference which should have been the real subject of the poem.

Much more compelling and infinitely more genuine is this poem's rival in celebrity, 'Stopping by Woods on a Snowy Evening', where the hesitation, the confrontation of the choice, is neither laboured nor inflated but on the contrary is sensitively dramatized in its own slight, fleeting terms. The woods *are* inviting – as death is, or escape is – but the hesitation is momentary; it pretends to be nothing more. And the enormously skilful ending, with the repetition of the last two lines catching the suddenly onward-going, duty-directed, hoofbeats of the horse, is again of precisely the right emotional and philosophic weight. The poem has embodied a faint, awesome, intimation.

The rather picturesque horse of 'Stopping by Woods' gave Frost a few moments worry but it is, for me, an unusually acceptable member of the poet's often rather twee and cosy bestiary. Frost's gentle way with animals is another feature of his charm. At his best, as in 'The Bear' and 'Two Meets Two', he is very good at catching the mutual, suspicious tentativeness with which animals encounter each other, and these chance meetings are made to carry with them, and in them, a sense of the mystery, the alien and tempting menace of nature as a whole. But here as always, Frost was prone to vulgarize and over-sell one of his best gifts. Thus one comes across the picture-book anthropomorphism of, say, the frogs in 'Pea Brush' or, worse still, the bird in 'The Wood-pile':

> A small bird flew before me. He was careful
> To put a tree between us when he lighted,
> And say no word to tell me who he was
> Who was so foolish as to think what *he* thought.

Having given at least a few reasons for Frost's popular appeal, the most important factor remains – and this has to do with the poet's promotion of himself – in his work – as an embodiment of a lost or threatened rural dream. Sceptics have been quick to point out that Frost only spent five years of his life actually working on the land, and his treacherous biographer has gone to some lengths to establish that Frost was never much good at farming anyway. But it doesn't seem to me that this is a very fruitful, or just, line of assault. The fact is that Frost did know what he was talking about when he talked of country matters – and his poetry is almost exclusively country-based. What *may* be said against him is that he made a bit too much of this knowledge, that there is an element of dressing up in dungarees about his work. Certainly it is the case that, although his poems mount much of their appeal on the illusion that here is a countryman talking to other countrymen, they are in fact aimed at an audience which is of the town. And for the townee, Frost's poems are marvellously full of helpful detail, both of country lore and also of the practicalities of farm labour. The sheer amount of detail rather gives the game away. To go back to 'Birches' – to the first half this time – one finds this:

> Soon the sun's warmth makes them shed crystal shells
> Shattering and avalanching on the snow crust –
> Such heaps of broken glass to sweep away
> You'd think the inner dome of heaven had fallen.
> They are dragged to the withered bracken by the load,
> And they seem not to break; though once they are bowed
> So low for long, they never right themselves:

It all gets to sound rather like a farm-training manual after a time, but the point is that there is nothing here – in terms of information – that even the most part-time countryman wouldn't know about. And nor is there much edge of excitement or visual beauty in the description – the lines hope to succeed by virtue of their useful factuality, their revelations about an alien mode of existence. Many of Frost's poems are full of lengthy, discursive slabs of pure informativeness – there is often nothing he likes more than wandering off into a chatty parenthesis about how this or that is fixed, how this or that tree or animal behaves. All of it music, of course, to the sluggish, guilty ears of urban America.

If these are some, at least, of the reasons for Frost's popularity, they are also some of the ingredients of his genuine excellence – I hope I've made my belief clear that the bad things in Frost are usually vulgarizations of the good. But this excellence had other aspects too – and very often the reverse side of Frost's charm was altogether uncharming. For example, Frost was popularly admired for his promotion of ideals of separateness, of self-reliance. Many of his nature poems concern the intrusion of one natural phenomenon upon another, and many of his lyric and dramatic poems present situations in which withdrawal, separation, standoffishness, are positively recommended. At his best, Frost's doctrines of self-reliance shaded into very moving confrontations of solitude, of alienation, of a low-spirited sense of exclusion, settling for tough, short-term objectives. Many of the poems in which Frost was truly and desolately himself are those which inhabit, stoically, a friendless realm.

The people along the sand
All turn and look one way.
They turn their back on the land.
They look at the sea all day.

As long as it takes to pass
A ship keeps raising its hull;
The wetter ground like glass
Reflects a standing gull.

The land may vary more;
But wherever the truth may be –
The water comes ashore,
And the people look at the sea.

They cannot look out far.
They cannot look in deep.
But when was that ever a bar
To any watch they keep?

It is difficult to imagine anything more terminally desolate than that. And yet the strain, the edginess, the intelligence of the poem derive really from a whole-hearted resistance to the terminal – a yearning for the conditions to be otherwise. And in some of Frost's finest poems about barriers and separations this wish is always formidably, futilely, present. But there are other poems in which something else, something more sinister, can be detected – indeed, cannot be ignored. I don't mean simply those right-wing poems of his later years in which he could complacently write:

I have none of the tenderer-than-thou
Collectivistic regimenting love
With which the modern world is being swept

nor those crude aphorisms in which he stated his philosophy to be 'Keep off each other and keep each other off'. The poems I'm thinking of are those, equally brutal in their way, but not in the least complacent, in which Frost faces – self-scrutinizingly – the point at which self-reliance is indistinguishable from self-centredness, from simple misanthropy. Typical of this strain is the dramatic poem, 'Out, Out –' in which a boy suffers from a bad sawmill accident. Frost describes the accident as follows:

His sister stood beside them in her apron
To tell them 'Supper.' At the word, the saw,
As if to prove saws knew what supper meant
Leaped out at the boy's hand, or seemed to leap . . .

The boy's death is recounted in similarly chilling terms:

They listened at his heart.
Little – less – nothing! – and that ended it.
No more to build on there. And they, since they
Were not the one dead, turned to their affairs.

There is a nerveless, anaesthetized cynicism here that one can only believe to be calculated and – in a subtle, disguising but revealing, sense – self-examining. It appears in almost equally bald form in poems like 'The Vanished Red' and 'The Self-Seeker'. In each of these the deliberate callousness, the anti-charm, is – Frost being Frost – of real importance, but there are other poems in which the poet allows matters to get even nearer home. Perhaps the most typical of these is the long work 'Home Burial'. This poem is, we now know, central to Frost's work because it is one of the very few directly autobiographical poems he wrote. Its subject is the death of a child. The mother, years after the child's death, is still in mourning and obscurely resents her husband having got over the whole thing so quickly. Frost's own first child died and his own wife was plagued with resentments and frustrations as a result. One might expect the poem, then, to be defensive or apologetic or at worst petulantly complaining. It is none of these things – unless one chooses to see the husband's resolute unfeelingness and self-involvement as constituting a very oblique kind of apologia. The fact is that throughout Frost's poems, women's fears and insecurities are treated with a fair amount of manly impatience – and 'Home Burial' wilfully carries that impatience to the point of a totally damaging blindness and insensitivity. We are never quite sure that Frost, having consciously and convincingly created this insensitivity, is at all interested in judging it. And yet he is the reverse of blind or insensitive to its *presence*.

And here is perhaps the most interesting of all the Frostian paradoxes: wholly alive to the ugly, unloving elements in his own nature, he now and then depicted these elements with maximum accuracy, without any self-forgiving glossing over or (what might have been more forgiving still) moralistic condemnation. Elsewhere, however, there is the spectacle of this same ugliness and unlovingness being transmuted into what have been applauded as courageous strengths. If one regards Frost's separatist doctrines as genuinely believed, and one has to, then a rather knotty conclusion tends to emerge: that Frost knew his own failings, knew what the world would think of them if it found out, and yet believed the world was wrong. Not only believed it, but devoted a whole career to proving it – in secret.

THE PASTURE

I'm going out to clean the pasture spring;
I'll only stop to rake the leaves away
(And wait to watch the water clear, I may):
I shan't be gone long. – You come too.

I'm going out to fetch the little calf
That's standing by the mother. It's so young
It totters when she licks it with her tongue.
I shan't be gone long. – You come too.

A BOY'S WILL

1913

INTO MY OWN

One of my wishes is that those dark trees,
So old and firm they scarcely show the breeze,
Were not, as 'twere, the merest mask of gloom,
But stretched away unto the edge of doom.

I should not be withheld but that some day
Into their vastness I should steal away,
Fearless of ever finding open land,
Or highway where the slow wheel pours the sand.

I do not see why I should e'er turn back,
Or those should not set forth upon my track
To overtake me, who should miss me here
And long to know if still I held them dear.

They would not find me changed from him they knew –
Only more sure of all I thought was true.

A LATE WALK

When I go up through the mowing field,
  The headless aftermath,
Smooth-laid like thatch with the heavy dew,
  Half closes the garden path.

And when I come to the garden ground,
  The whir of sober birds
Up from the tangle of withered weeds
  Is sadder than any words.

A tree beside the wall stands bare,
  But a leaf that lingered brown,

Disturbed, I doubt not, by my thought,
  Comes softly rattling down.

I end not far from my going forth,
  By picking the faded blue
Of the last remaining aster flower
  To carry again to you.

STARS

How countlessly they congregate
  O'er our tumultuous snow,
Which flows in shapes as tall as trees
  When wintry winds do blow! –

As if with keenness for our fate,
  Our faltering few steps on
To white rest, and a place of rest
  Invisible at dawn –

And yet with neither love nor hate,
  Those stars like some snow-white
Minerva's snow-white marble eyes
  Without the gift of sight.

STORM FEAR

When the wind works against us in the dark,
And pelts with snow
The lower-chamber window on the east,
And whispers with a sort of stifled bark,
The beast,
'Come out! Come out!' –
It costs no inward struggle not to go,

Ah, no!
I count our strength,
Two and a child,
Those of us not asleep subdued to mark
How the cold creeps as the fire dies at length –
How drifts are piled,
Dooryard and road ungraded,
Till even the comforting barn grows far away,
And my heart owns a doubt
Whether 'tis in us to arise with day
And save ourselves unaided.

FLOWER-GATHERING

I left you in the morning,
And in the morning glow
You walked a way beside me
To make me sad to go.
Do you know me in the gloaming,
Gaunt and dusty gray with roaming?
Are you dumb because you know me not,
Or dumb because you know?

All for me? And not a question
For the faded flowers gay
That could take me from beside you
For the ages of a day?
They are yours, and be the measure
Of their worth for you to treasure,
The measure of the little while
That I've been long away.

WAITING

Afield at dusk

What things for dream there are when specter-like,
Moving among tall haycocks lightly piled,
I enter alone upon the stubble field,
From which the laborers' voices late have died,
And in the antiphony of afterglow
And rising full moon, sit me down
Upon the full moon's side of the first haycock
And lose myself amid so many alike.

I dream upon the opposing lights of the hour,
Preventing shadow until the moon prevail;
I dream upon the nighthawks peopling heaven,
Each circling each with vague unearthly cry,
Or plunging headlong with fierce twang afar;
And on the bat's mute antics, who would seem
Dimly to have made out my secret place,
Only to lose it when he pirouettes,
And seek it endlessly with purblind haste;
On the last swallow's sweep; and on the rasp
In the abyss of odor and rustle at my back,
That, silenced by my advent, finds once more,
After an interval, his instrument,
And tries once – twice – and thrice if I be there;
And on the worn book of old-golden song
I brought not here to read, it seems, but hold
And freshen in this air of withering sweetness;
But on the memory of one absent, most,
For whom these lines when they shall greet her eye.

A DREAM PANG

I had withdrawn in forest, and my song
Was swallowed up in leaves that blew alway;
And to the forest edge you came one day
(This was my dream) and looked and pondered long,
But did not enter, though the wish was strong:
You shook your pensive head as who should say,
'I dare not – too far in his footsteps stray –
He must seek me would he undo the wrong.'

Not far, but near, I stood and saw it all,
Behind low boughs the trees let down outside;
And the sweet pang it cost me not to call
And tell you that I saw does still abide.
But 'tis not true that thus I dwelt aloof,
For the wood wakes, and you are here for proof.

IN NEGLECT

They leave us so to the way we took,
As two in whom they were proved mistaken,
That we sit sometimes in the wayside nook,
With mischievous, vagrant, seraphic look,
And *try* if we cannot feel forsaken.

THE VANTAGE POINT

If tired of trees I seek again mankind,
Well I know where to hie me – in the dawn,
To a slope where the cattle keep the lawn.
There amid lolling juniper reclined,
Myself unseen, I see in white defined

Far off the homes of men, and farther still,
The graves of men on an opposing hill,
Living or dead, whichever are to mind.

And if by noon I have too much of these,
I have but to turn on my arm, and lo,
The sunburned hillside sets my face aglow,
My breathing shakes the bluet like a breeze,
I smell the earth, I smell the bruisèd plant,
I look into the crater of the ant.

MOWING

There was never a sound beside the wood but one,
And that was my long scythe whispering to the ground.
What was it it whispered? I knew not well myself;
Perhaps it was something about the heat of the sun,
Something, perhaps, about the lack of sound –
And that was why it whispered and did not speak.
It was no dream of the gift of idle hours,
Or easy gold at the hand of fay or elf:
Anything more than the truth would have seemed too weak
To the earnest love that laid the swale in rows,
Not without feeble-pointed spikes of flowers
(Pale orchises), and scared a bright green snake.
The fact is the sweetest dream that labor knows.
My long scythe whispered and left the hay to make.

GOING FOR WATER

The well was dry beside the door,
And so we went with pail and can
Across the fields behind the house
To seek the brook if still it ran;

Not loth to have excuse to go,
  Because the autumn eve was fair
(Though chill), because the fields were ours,
  And by the brook our woods were there.

We ran as if to meet the moon
  That slowly dawned behind the trees,
The barren boughs without the leaves,
  Without the birds, without the breeze.

But once within the wood, we paused
  Like gnomes that hid us from the moon,
Ready to run to hiding new
  With laughter when she found us soon.

Each laid on other a staying hand
  To listen ere we dared to look,
And in the hush we joined to make
  We heard, we knew we heard the brook.

A note as from a single place,
  A slender tinkling fall that made
Now drops that floated on the pool
  Like pearls, and now a silver blade.

THE TUFT OF FLOWERS

I went to turn the grass once after one
Who mowed it in the dew before the sun.

The dew was gone that made his blade so keen
Before I came to view the leveled scene.

I looked for him behind an isle of trees;
I listened for his whetstone on the breeze.

But he had gone his way, the grass all mown,
And I must be, as he had been – alone,

'As all must be,' I said within my heart,
'Whether they work together or apart.'

But as I said it, swift there passed me by
On noiseless wing a bewildered butterfly,

Seeking with memories grown dim o'er night
Some resting flower of yesterday's delight.

And once I marked his flight go round and round,
As where some flower lay withering on the ground.

And then he flew as far as eye could see,
And then on tremulous wing came back to me.

I thought of questions that have no reply,
And would have turned to toss the grass to dry;

But he turned first, and led my eye to look
At a tall tuft of flowers beside a brook,

A leaping tongue of bloom the scythe had spared
Beside a reedy brook the scythe had bared.

The mower in the dew had loved them thus,
By leaving them to flourish, not for us,

Nor yet to draw one thought of ours to him,
But from sheer morning gladness at the brim.

The butterfly and I had lit upon,
Nevertheless, a message from the dawn,

That made me hear the wakening birds around,
And hear his long scythe whispering to the ground,

And feel a spirit kindred to my own;
So that henceforth I worked no more alone;

But glad with him, I worked as with his aid,
And weary, sought at noon with him the shade;

And dreaming, as it were, held brotherly speech
With one whose thought I had not hoped to reach.

'Men work together,' I told him from the heart,
'Whether they work together or apart.'

NOW CLOSE THE WINDOWS

Now close the windows and hush all the fields:
  If the trees must, let them silently toss;
No bird is singing now, and if there is,
  Be it my loss.

It will be long ere the marshes resume,
  It will be long ere the earliest bird:
So close the windows and not hear the wind,
  But see all wind-stirred.

IN HARDWOOD GROVES

The same leaves over and over again!
They fall from giving shade above,
To make one texture of faded brown
And fit the earth like a leather glove.

Before the leaves can mount again
To fill the trees with another shade,
They must go down past things coming up.
They must go down into the dark decayed.

They *must* be pierced by flowers and put
Beneath the feet of dancing flowers.
However it is in some other world
I know that this is the way in ours.

OCTOBER

O hushed October morning mild,
Thy leaves have ripened to the fall;
Tomorrow's wind, if it be wild,
Should waste them all.
The crows above the forest call;
Tomorrow they may form and go.
O hushed October morning mild,
Begin the hours of this day slow.
Make the day seem to us less brief.
Hearts not averse to being beguiled,
Beguile us in the way you know.
Release one leaf at break of day;
At noon release another leaf;
One from our trees, one far away,
Retard the sun with gentle mist;
Enchant the land with amethyst.
Slow, slow!
For the grapes' sake, if they were all,
Whose leaves already are burnt with frost,
Whose clustered fruit must else be lost –
For the grapes' sake along the wall.

RELUCTANCE

Out through the fields and the woods
  And over the walls I have wended;
I have climbed the hills of view
  And looked at the world, and descended;
I have come by the highway home,
  And lo, it is ended.

The leaves are all dead on the ground,
  Save those that the oak is keeping
To ravel them one by one
  And let them go scraping and creeping
Out over the crusted snow,
  When others are sleeping.

And the dead leaves lie huddled and still,
  No longer blown hither and thither;
The last lone aster is gone;
  The flowers of the witch hazel wither;
The heart is still aching to seek,
  But the feet question 'Whither?'

Ah, when to the heart of man
  Was it ever less than a treason
To go with the drift of things,
  To yield with a grace to reason,
And bow and accept the end
  Of a love or a season?

NORTH OF BOSTON

1914

MENDING WALL

Something there is that doesn't love a wall,
That sends the frozen-ground-swell under it
And spills the upper boulders in the sun,
And makes gaps even two can pass abreast.
The work of hunters is another thing:
I have come after them and made repair
Where they have left not one stone on a stone,
But they would have the rabbit out of hiding,
To please the yelping dogs. The gaps I mean,
No one has seen them made or heard them made,
But at spring mending-time we find them there.
I let my neighbor know beyond the hill;
And on a day we meet to walk the line
And set the wall between us once again.
We keep the wall between us as we go.
To each the boulders that have fallen to each.
And some are loaves and some so nearly balls
We have to use a spell to make them balance:
'Stay where you are until our backs are turned!'
We wear our fingers rough with handling them.
Oh, just another kind of outdoor game,
One on a side. It comes to little more:
There where it is we do not need the wall:
He is all pine and I am apple orchard.
My apple trees will never get across
And eat the cones under his pines, I tell him.
He only says, 'Good fences make good neighbors.'
Spring is the mischief in me, and I wonder
If I could put a notion in his head:
'*Why* do they make good neighbors? Isn't it
Where there are cows? But here there are no cows.

Before I built a wall I'd ask to know
What I was walling in or walling out,
And to whom I was like to give offense.
Something there is that doesn't love a wall,
That wants it down.' I could say 'Elves' to him,
But it's not elves exactly, and I'd rather
He said it for himself. I see him there,
Bringing a stone grasped firmly by the top
In each hand, like an old-stone savage armed.
He moves in darkness as it seems to me,
Not of woods only and the shade of trees.
He will not go behind his father's saying,
And he likes having thought of it so well
He says again, 'Good fences make good neighbors.'

THE DEATH OF THE HIRED MAN

Mary sat musing on the lamp-flame at the table,
Waiting for Warren. When she heard his step,
She ran on tiptoe down the darkened passage
To meet him in the doorway with the news
And put him on his guard. 'Silas is back.'
She pushed him outward with her through the door
And shut it after her. 'Be kind,' she said.
She took the market things from Warren's arms
And set them on the porch, then drew him down
To sit beside her on the wooden steps.

'When was I ever anything but kind to him?
But I'll not have the fellow back,' he said.
'I told him so last haying, didn't I?
If he left then, I said, that ended it.
What good is he? Who else will harbor him
At his age for the little he can do?
What help he is there's no depending on.

Off he goes always when I need him most.
He thinks he ought to earn a little pay,
Enough at least to buy tobacco with,
So he won't have to beg and be beholden.
"All right," I say, "I can't afford to pay
Any fixed wages, though I wish I could."
"Someone else can." "Then someone else will have to."
I shouldn't mind his bettering himself
If that was what it was. You can be certain,
When he begins like that, there's someone at him
Trying to coax him off with pocket money –
In haying time, when any help is scarce.
In winter he comes back to us. I'm done.'

'Sh! not so loud: he'll hear you,' Mary said.

'I want him to: he'll have to soon or late.'

'He's worn out. He's asleep beside the stove.
When I came up from Rowe's I found him here,
Huddled against the barn door fast asleep,
A miserable sight, and frightening, too –
You needn't smile – I didn't recognize him –
I wasn't looking for him – and he's changed.
Wait till you see.'

'Where did you say he'd been?'

'He didn't say. I dragged him to the house,
And gave him tea and tried to make him smoke.
I tried to make him talk about his travels.
Nothing would do: he just kept nodding off.'

'What did he say? Did he say anything?'

'But little.'

'Anything? Mary, confess
He said he'd come to ditch the meadow for me.'

'Warren!'

'But did he? I just want to know.'

'Of course he did. What would you have him say?
Surely you wouldn't grudge the poor old man
Some humble way to save his self-respect.
He added, if you really care to know,
He meant to clear the upper pasture, too.
That sounds like something you have heard before?
Warren, I wish you could have heard the way
He jumbled everything. I stopped to look
Two or three times – he made me feel so queer –
To see if he was talking in his sleep.
He ran on Harold Wilson – you remember –
The boy you had in haying four years since.
He's finished school, and teaching in his college.
Silas declares you'll have to get him back.
He says they two will make a team for work:
Between them they will lay this farm as smooth!
The way he mixed that in with other things.
He thinks young Wilson a likely lad, though daft
On education – you know how they fought
All through July under the blazing sun,
Silas up on the cart to build the load,
Harold along beside to pitch it on.'

'Yes, I took care to keep well out of earshot.'

'Well, those days trouble Silas like a dream.
You wouldn't think they would. How some things linger!
Harold's young college-boy's assurance piqued him.
And so many years he still keeps finding
Good arguments he sees he might have used.
I sympathize. I know just how it feels
To think of the right thing to say too late.
Harold's associated in his mind with Latin.
He asked me what I thought of Harold's saying
He studied Latin, like the violin,

Because he liked it – that an argument!
He said he couldn't make the boy believe
He could find water with a hazel prong –
Which showed how much good school had ever done him.
He wanted to go over that. But most of all
He thinks if he could have another chance
To teach him how to build a load of hay –'

'I know, that's Silas' one accomplishment.
He bundles every forkful in its place,
And tags and numbers it for future reference,
So he can find and easily dislodge it
In the unloading. Silas does that well.
He takes it out in bunches like big birds' nests.
You never see him standing on the hay
He's trying to lift, straining to lift himself.'

'He thinks if he could teach him that, he'd be
Some good perhaps to someone in the world.
He hates to see a boy the fool of books.
Poor Silas, so concerned for other folk,
And nothing to look backward to with pride,
And nothing to look forward to with hope,
So now and never any different.'

Part of a moon was falling down the west,
Dragging the whole sky with it to the hills.
Its light poured softly in her lap. She saw it
And spread her apron to it. She put out her hand
Among the harplike morning-glory strings,
Taut with the dew from garden bed to eaves,
As if she played unheard some tenderness
That wrought on him beside her in the night.
'Warren,' she said, 'he has come home to die:
You needn't be afraid he'll leave you this time.'

'Home,' he mocked gently.

'Yes, what else but home?
It all depends on what you mean by home.
Of course he's nothing to us, any more
Than was the hound that came a stranger to us
Out of the woods, worn out upon the trail.'

'Home is the place where, when you have to go there,
They have to take you in.'

'I should have called it
Something you somehow haven't to deserve.'

Warren leaned out and took a step or two,
Picked up a little stick, and brought it back
And broke it in his hand and tossed it by.
'Silas has better claim on us you think
Than on his brother? Thirteen little miles
As the road winds would bring him to his door.
Silas has walked that far no doubt today.
Why doesn't he go there? His brother's rich,
A somebody – director in the bank.'

'He never told us that.'

'We know it, though.'

'I think his brother ought to help, of course.
I'll see to that if there is need. He ought of right
To take him in, and might be willing to –
He may be better than appearances.
But have some pity on Silas. Do you think
If he had any pride in claiming kin
Or anything he looked for from his brother,
He'd keep so still about him all this time?'

'I wonder what's between them.'

'I can tell you.
Silas is what he is – we wouldn't mind him –

But just the kind that kinsfolk can't abide.
He never did a thing so very bad.
He don't know why he isn't quite as good
As anybody. Worthless though he is,
He won't be made ashamed to please his brother.'

'*I* can't think Si ever hurt anyone.'

'No, but he hurt my heart the way he lay
And rolled his old head on that sharp-edged chair-back.
He wouldn't let me put him on the lounge.
You must go in and see what you can do.
I made the bed up for him there tonight.
You'll be surprised at him – how much he's broken.
His working days are done; I'm sure of it.'

'I'd not be in a hurry to say that.'

'I haven't been. Go, look, see for yourself.
But, Warren, please remember how it is:
He's come to help you ditch the meadow.
He has a plan. You mustn't laugh at him.
He may not speak of it, and then he may.
I'll sit and see if that small sailing cloud
Will hit or miss the moon.'

It hit the moon.
Then there were three there, making a dim row,
The moon, the little silver cloud, and she.

Warren returned – too soon, it seemed to her –
Slipped to her side, caught up her hand and waited.

'Warren?' she questioned.

'Dead,' was all he answered.

The mountain held the town as in a shadow.
I saw so much before I slept there once:
I noticed that I missed stars in the west,
Where its black body cut into the sky.
Near me it seemed: I felt it like a wall
Behind which I was sheltered from a wind.
And yet between the town and it I found,
When I walked forth at dawn to see new things,
Were fields, a river, and beyond, more fields.
The river at the time was fallen away,
And made a widespread brawl on cobblestones;
But the signs showed what it had done in spring:
Good grassland gullied out, and in the grass
Ridges of sand, and driftwood stripped of bark.
I crossed the river and swung round the mountain.
And there I met a man who moved so slow
With white-faced oxen, in a heavy cart,
It seemed no harm to stop him altogether.

'What town is this?' I asked.

'This? Lunenburg.'

Then I was wrong: the town of my sojourn,
Beyond the bridge, was not that of the mountain,
But only felt at night its shadowy presence.
'Where is your village? Very far from here?'

'There is no village – only scattered farms.
We were but sixty voters last election.
We can't in nature grow to many more:
That thing takes all the room!' He moved his goad.
The mountain stood there to be pointed at.

Pasture ran up the side a little way,
And then there was a wall of trees with trunks;

After that only tops of trees, and cliffs
Imperfectly concealed among the leaves.
A dry ravine emerged from under boughs
Into the pasture.

'That looks like a path.
Is that the way to reach the top from here? –
Not for this morning, but some other time:
I must be getting back to breakfast now.'

'I don't advise your trying from this side.
There is no proper path, but those that *have*
Been up, I understand, have climbed from Ladd's.
That's five miles back. You can't mistake the place:
They logged it there last winter some way up.
I'd take you, but I'm bound the other way.'

'You've never climbed it?"

'I've been on the sides,
Deer-hunting and trout-fishing. There's a brook
That starts up on it somewhere – I've heard say
Right on the top, tip-top – a curious thing.
But what would interest you about the brook,
It's always cold in summer, warm in winter.
One of the great sights going is to see
It steam in winter like an ox's breath,
Until the bushes all along its banks
Are inch-deep with the frosty spines and bristles –
You know the kind. Then let the sun shine on it!'

'There ought to be a view around the world
From such a mountain – if it isn't wooded
Clear to the top.' I saw through leafy screens
Great granite terraces in sun and shadow,
Shelves one could rest a knee on getting up –
With depths behind him sheer a hundred feet –
Or turn and sit on and look out and down,

With little ferns in crevices at his elbow.

'As to that I can't say. But there's the spring,
Right on the summit, almost like a fountain.
That ought to be worth seeing.'

'If it's there.

You never saw it?'

'I guess there's no doubt
About its being there. I never saw it.
It may not be right on the very top:
It wouldn't have to be a long way down
To have some head of water from above,
And a *good distance* down might not be noticed
By anyone who'd come a long way up.
One time I asked a fellow climbing it
To look and tell me later how it was.'

'What did he say?'

'He said there was a lake
Somewhere in Ireland on a mountain top.'

'But a lake's different. What about the spring?'

'He never got up high enough to see.
That's why I don't advise your trying this side.
He tried this side. I've always meant to go
And look myself, but you know how it is:
It doesn't seem so much to climb a mountain
You've worked around the foot of all your life.
What would I do? Go in my overalls,
With a big stick, the same as when the cows
Haven't come down to the bars at milking time?
Or with a shotgun for a stray black bear?
'Twouldn't seem real to climb for climbing it.'

'I shouldn't climb it if I didn't want to –
Not for the sake of climbing. What's its name?'

'We call it Hor: I don't know if that's right.'

'Can one walk around it? Would it be too far?'

'You can drive round and keep in Lunenburg,
But it's as much as ever you can do,
The boundary lines keep in so close to it.
Hor is the township, and the township's Hor –
And a few houses sprinkled round the foot,
Like boulders broken off the upper cliff,
Rolled out a little farther than the rest.'

'Warm in December, cold in June, you say?'

'I don't suppose the water's changed at all.
You and I know enough to know it's warm
Compared with cold, and cold compared with warm.
But all the fun's in how you say a thing.'

'You've lived here all your life?'

'Ever since Hor
Was no bigger than a —' What, I did not hear.
He drew the oxen toward him with light touches
Of his slim goad on nose and offside flank,
Gave them their marching orders and was moving.

A HUNDRED COLLARS

Lancaster bore him – such a little town,
Such a great man. It doesn't see him often
Of late years, though he keeps the old homestead
And sends the children down there with their mother
To run wild in the summer – a little wild.
Sometimes he joins them for a day or two
And sees old friends he somehow can't get near.
They meet him in the general store at night,
Preoccupied with formidable mail,

Rifling a printed letter as he talks.
They seem afraid. He wouldn't have it so:
Though a great scholar, he's a democrat,
If not at heart, at least on principle.

Lately when coming up to Lancaster,
His train being late, he missed another train
And had four hours to wait at Woodsville Junction
After eleven o'clock at night. Too tired
To think of sitting such an ordeal out,
He turned to the hotel to find a bed.

'No room,' the night clerk said. 'Unless —'

Woodsville's a place of shrieks and wandering lamps
And cars that shock and rattle – and *one* hotel.

'You say "unless."'

'Unless you wouldn't mind

Sharing a room with someone else.'

'Who is it?'

'A man.'

'So I should hope. What kind of man?'

'I know him: he's all right. A man's a man.
Separate beds, of course, you understand.'
The night clerk blinked his eyes and dared him on.

'Who's that man sleeping in the office chair?
Has he had the refusal of my chance?'

'He was afraid of being robbed or murdered.
What do you say?'

'I'll have to have a bed.'

The night clerk led him up three flights of stairs
And down a narrow passage full of doors,
At the last one of which he knocked and entered.
'Lafe, here's a fellow wants to share your room.'

'Show him this way. I'm not afraid of him.
I'm not so drunk I can't take care of myself.'

The night clerk clapped a bedstead on the foot.
'This will be yours. Good-night,' he said, and went.

'Lafe was the name, I think?'
'Yes, *Lay*fayette.
You got it the first time. And yours?'
'Magoon.
Doctor Magoon.'
'A Doctor?'
'Well, a teacher.'

'Professor Square-the-circle-till-you're-tired?
Hold on, there's something I don't think of now
That I had on my mind to ask the first
Man that knew anything I happened in with.
I'll ask you later – don't let me forget it.'

The Doctor looked at Lafe and looked away.
A man? A brute. Naked above the waist.
He sat there creased and shining in the light,
Fumbling the buttons in a well-starched shirt.
'I'm moving into a size-larger shirt.
I've felt mean lately; mean's no name for it.
I just found what the matter was tonight:
I've been a-choking like a nursery tree
When it outgrows the wire band of its name tag.
I blamed it on the hot spell we've been having.
'Twas nothing but my foolish hanging back,
Not liking to own up I'd grown a size.
Number eighteen this is. What size do you wear?'

The Doctor caught his throat convulsively.
'Oh – ah – fourteen – fourteen.'
'Fourteen! You say so!

I can remember when I wore fourteen.
And come to think I must have back at home
More than a hundred collars, size fourteen.
Too bad to waste them all. You ought to have them.
They're yours and welcome; let me send them to you. –
What makes you stand there on one leg like that?
You're not much furtherer than where Kike left you.
You act as if you wished you hadn't come.
Sit down or lie down, friend; you make me nervous.'

The Doctor made a subdued dash for it,
And propped himself at bay against a pillow.

'Not that way, with your shoes on Kike's white bed.
You can't rest that way. Let me pull your shoes off.'

'Don't touch me, please – I say, don't touch me, please.
I'll not be put to bed by you, my man.'

'Just as you say. Have it your own way, then.
"My man" is it? You talk like a professor.
Speaking of who's afraid of who, however,
I'm thinking I have more to lose than you
If anything should happen to be wrong.
Who wants to cut your number fourteen throat!
Let's have a showdown as an evidence
Of good faith. There is ninety dollars.
Come, if you're not afraid.'

'*I*'m not afraid.
There's five: that's all I carry.'

'I can search you?
Where are you moving over to? Stay still.
You'd better tuck your money under you
And sleep on it, the way I always do
When I'm with people I don't trust at night.'

'Will you believe me if I put it there
Right on the counterpane – that I do trust you?'

'You'd say so, Mister Man. – I'm a collector.
My ninety isn't mine – you won't think that.
I pick it up a dollar at a time
All round the country for the *Weekly News*,
Published in Bow. You know the *Weekly News*?'

'Known it since I was young.'

'Then you know me.
Now we are getting on together – talking.
I'm sort of Something for it at the front.
My business is to find what people want:
They pay for it, and so they ought to have it.
Fairbanks, he says to me – he's editor –
"Feel out the public sentiment" – he says.
A good deal comes on me when all is said.
The only trouble is we disagree
In politics: I'm Vermont Democrat –
You know what that is, sort of double-dyed;
The *News* has always been Republican.
Fairbanks, he says to me, "Help us this year,"
Meaning by us their ticket. "No," I says,
"I can't and won't. You've been in long enough:
It's time you turned around and boosted us.
You'll have to pay me more than ten a week
If I'm expected to elect Bill Taft.
I doubt if I could do it anyway."'

'You seem to shape the paper's policy.'

'You see I'm in with everybody, know 'em all.
I almost know their farms as well as they do.'

'You drive around? It must be pleasant work.'

'It's business, but I can't say it's not fun.
What I like best's the lay of different farms,

Coming out on them from a stretch of woods,
Or over a hill or round a sudden corner.
I like to find folks getting out in spring,
Raking the dooryard, working near the house.
Later they get out further in the fields.
Everything's shut sometimes except the barn;
The family's all away in some back meadow.
There's a hay load a-coming – when it comes.
And later still they all get driven in:
The fields are stripped to lawn, the garden patches
Stripped to bare ground, the maple trees
To whips and poles. There's nobody about.
The chimney, though, keeps up a good brisk smoking.
And I lie back and ride. I take the reins
Only when someone's coming, and the mare
Stops when she likes: I tell her when to go.
I've spoiled Jemima in more ways than one.
She's got so she turns in at every house
As if she had some sort of curvature,
No matter if I have no errand there.
She thinks I'm sociable. I maybe am.
It's seldom I get down except for meals, though.
Folks entertain me from the kitchen doorstep,
All in a family row down to the youngest.'

'One would suppose they might not be as glad
To see you as you are to see them.'

'Oh,
Because I want their dollar? I don't want
Anything they've not got. I never dun.
I'm there, and they can pay me if they like.
I go nowhere on purpose: I happen by. –
Sorry there is no cup to give you a drink.
I drink out of the bottle – not your style.
Mayn't I offer you –?'

'No, no, no, thank you.'

'Just as you say. Here's looking at you, then. –
And now I'm leaving you a little while.
You'll rest easier when I'm gone, perhaps –
Lie down – let yourself go and get some sleep.
But first – let's see – what was I going to ask you?
Those collars – who shall I address them to,
Suppose you aren't awake when I come back?'

'Really, friend, I can't let you. You – may need them.'

'Not till I shrink, when they'll be out of style.'

'But really I – I have so many collars.'

'I don't know who I rather would have have them.
They're only turning yellow where they are.
But you're the doctor, as the saying is.
I'll put the light out. Don't you wait for me:
I've just begun the night. You get some sleep.
I'll knock so-fashion and peep round the door
When I come back, so you'll know who it is.
There's nothing I'm afraid of like scared people.
I don't want you should shoot me in the head. –
What am I doing carrying off this bottle? –
There now, you get some sleep.'

He shut the door.
The Doctor slid a little down the pillow.

HOME BURIAL

He saw her from the bottom of the stairs
Before she saw him. She was starting down,
Looking back over her shoulder at some fear.
She took a doubtful step and then undid it
To raise herself and look again. He spoke

Advancing toward her: 'What is it you see
From up there always? – for I want to know.'
She turned and sank upon her skirts at that,
And her face changed from terrified to dull.
He said to gain time: 'What is it you see?'
Mounting until she cowered under him.
'I will find out now – you must tell me, dear.'
She, in her place, refused him any help,
With the least stiffening of her neck and silence.
She let him look, sure that he wouldn't see,
Blind creature; and awhile he didn't see.
But at last he murmured, 'Oh,' and again, 'Oh.'

'What is it – what?' she said.

'Just that I see.'

'You don't,' she challenged. 'Tell me what it is.'

'The wonder is I didn't see at once.
I never noticed it from here before.
I must be wonted to it – that's the reason.
The little graveyard where my people are!
So small the window frames the whole of it.
Not so much larger than a bedroom, is it?
There are three stones of slate and one of marble,
Broad-shouldered little slabs there in the sunlight
On the sidehill. We haven't to mind *those*.
But I understand: it is not the stones,
But the child's mound —'

'Don't, don't, don't,

don't,' she cried.

She withdrew, shrinking from beneath his arm
That rested on the banister, and slid downstairs;
And turned on him with such a daunting look,
He said twice over before he knew himself:
'Can't a man speak of his own child he's lost?'

'Not you! – Oh, where's my hat? Oh, I don't need it!
I must get out of here. I must get air. –
I don't know rightly whether any man can.'

'Amy! Don't go to someone else this time.
Listen to me. I won't come down the stairs.'
He sat and fixed his chin between his fists.
'There's something I should like to ask you, dear.'

'You don't know how to ask it.'

'Help me, then.'

Her fingers moved the latch for all reply.

'My words are nearly always an offense.
I don't know how to speak of anything
So as to please you. But I might be taught,
I should suppose. I can't say I see how.
A man must partly give up being a man
With womenfolk. We could have some arrangement
By which I'd bind myself to keep hands off
Anything special you're a-mind to name.
Though I don't like such things 'twixt those that love.
Two that don't love can't live together without them.
But two that do can't live together with them.'
She moved the latch a little. 'Don't – don't go.
Don't carry it to someone else this time.
Tell me about it if it's something human.
Let me into your grief. I'm not so much
Unlike other folks as your standing there
Apart would make me out. Give me my chance.
I do think, though, you overdo it a little.
What was it brought you up to think it the thing
To take your mother-loss of a first child
So inconsolably – in the face of love.
You'd think his memory might be satisfied —'

'There you go sneering now!'

'I'm not, I'm not!
You make me angry. I'll come down to you.
God, what a woman! And it's come to this,
A man can't speak of his own child that's dead.'

'You can't because you don't know how to speak.
If you had any feelings, you that dug
With your own hand – how could you? – his little grave;
I saw you from that very window there,
Making the gravel leap and leap in air,
Leap up, like that, like that, and land so lightly
And roll back down the mound beside the hole.
I thought, Who is that man? I didn't know you.
And I crept down the stairs and up the stairs
To look again, and still your spade kept lifting.
Then you came in. I heard your rumbling voice
Out in the kitchen, and I don't know why,
But I went near to see with my own eyes.
You could sit there with the stains on your shoes
Of the fresh earth from your own baby's grave
And talk about your everyday concerns.
You had stood the spade up against the wall
Outside there in the entry, for I saw it.'

'I shall laugh the worst laugh I ever laughed.
I'm cursed. God, if I don't believe I'm cursed.'

'I can repeat the very words you were saying:
"Three foggy mornings and one rainy day
Will rot the best birch fence a man can build."
Think of it, talk like that at such a time!
What had how long it takes a birch to rot
To do with what was in the darkened parlor?
You *couldn't* care! The nearest friends can go
With anyone to death, comes so far short
They might as well not try to go at all.
No, from the time when one is sick to death,

One is alone, and he dies more alone.
Friends make pretense of following to the grave,
But before one is in it, their minds are turned
And making the best of their way back to life
And living people, and things they understand.
But the world's evil. I won't have grief so
If I can change it. Oh, I won't, I won't!'

'There, you have said it all and you feel better.
You won't go now. You're crying. Close the door.
The heart's gone out of it: why keep it up?
Amy! There's someone coming down the road!'

'*You* – oh, you think the talk is all. I must go –
Somewhere out of this house. How can I make you —'

'If – you – do!' She was opening the door wider.
'Where do you mean to go? First tell me that.
I'll follow and bring you back by force. I *will*! –'

A SERVANT TO SERVANTS

I didn't make you know how glad I was
To have you come and camp here on our land.
I promised myself to get down some day
And see the way you lived, but I don't know!
With a houseful of hungry men to feed
I guess you'd find. . . . It seems to me
I can't express my feelings, any more
Than I can raise my voice or want to lift
My hand (oh, I can lift it when I have to).
Did ever you feel so? I hope you never.
It's got so I don't even know for sure
Whether I *am* glad, sorry, or anything.
There's nothing but a voice-like left inside
That seems to tell me how I ought to feel,

And would feel if I wasn't all gone wrong.
You take the lake. I look and look at it.
I see it's a fair, pretty sheet of water.
I stand and make myself repeat out loud
The advantages it has, so long and narrow,
Like a deep piece of some old running river
Cut short off at both ends. It lies five miles
Straightaway through the mountain notch
From the sink window where I wash the plates,
And all our storms come up toward the house,
Drawing the slow waves whiter and whiter and whiter.
It took my mind off doughnuts and soda biscuit
To step outdoors and take the water dazzle
A sunny morning, or take the rising wind
About my face and body and through my wrapper,
When a storm threatened from the Dragon's Den,
And a cold chill shivered across the lake.
I see it's a fair, pretty sheet of water,
Our Willoughby! How did you hear of it?
I expect, though, everyone's heard of it.
In a book about ferns? Listen to that!
You let things more like feathers regulate
Your going and coming. And you like it here?
I can see how you might. But I don't know!
It would be different if more people came,
For then there would be business. As it is,
The cottages Len built, sometimes we rent them,
Sometimes we don't. We've a good piece of shore
That ought to be worth something, and may yet.
But I don't count on it as much as Len.
He looks on the bright side of everything,
Including me. He thinks I'll be all right
With doctoring. But it's not medicine –
Lowe is the only doctor's dared to say so –
It's rest I want – there, I have said it out –

From cooking meals for hungry hired men
And washing dishes after them – from doing
Things over and over that just won't stay done.
By good rights I ought not to have so much
Put on me, but there seems no other way.
Len says one steady pull more ought to do it.
He says the best way out is always through.
And I agree to that, or in so far
As that I can see no way out but through –
Leastways for me – and then they'll be convinced.
It's not that Len don't want the best for me.
It was his plan our moving over in
Beside the lake from where that day I showed you
We used to live – ten miles from anywhere.
We didn't change without some sacrifice,
But Len went at it to make up the loss.
His work's a man's, of course, from sun to sun,
But he works when he works as hard as I do –
Though there's small profit in comparisons.
(Women and men will make them all the same.)
But work ain't all. Len undertakes too much.
He's into everything in town. This year
It's highways, and he's got too many men
Around him to look after that make waste.
They take advantage of him shamefully,
And proud, too, of themselves for doing so.
We have four here to board, great good-for-nothings,
Sprawling about the kitchen with their talk
While I fry their bacon. Much they care!
No more put out in what they do or say
Than if I wasn't in the room at all.
Coming and going all the time, they are:
I don't learn what their names are, let alone
Their characters, or whether they are safe
To have inside the house with doors unlocked.

I'm not afraid of them, though, if they're not
Afraid of me. There's two can play at that.
I have my fancies: it runs in the family.
My father's brother wasn't right. They kept him
Locked up for years back there at the old farm.
I've been away once – yes, I've been away.
The State Asylum. I was prejudiced;
I wouldn't have sent anyone of mine there;
You know the old idea – the only asylum
Was the poorhouse, and those who could afford,
Rather than send their folks to such a place,
Kept them at home; and it does seem more human.
But it's not so: the place is the asylum.
There they have every means proper to do with,
And you aren't darkening other people's lives –
Worse than no good to them, and they no good
To you in your condition; you can't know
Affection or the want of it in that state.
I've heard too much of the old-fashioned way.
My father's brother, he went mad quite young.
Some thought he had been bitten by a dog,
Because his violence took on the form
Of carrying his pillow in his teeth;
But it's more likely he was crossed in love,
Or so the story goes. It was some girl.
Anyway all he talked about was love.
They soon saw he would do someone a mischief
If he wa'n't kept strict watch of, and it ended
In father's building him a sort of cage,
Or room within a room, of hickory poles,
Like stanchions in the barn, from floor to ceiling –
A narrow passage all the way around.
Anything they put in for furniture
He'd tear to pieces, even a bed to lie on.
So they made the place comfortable with straw.

Like a beast's stall, to ease their consciences.
Of course they had to feed him without dishes.
They tried to keep him clothed, but he paraded
With his clothes on his arm – all of his clothes.
Cruel – it sounds. I s'pose they did the best
They knew. And just when he was at the height,
Father and mother married, and mother came,
A bride, to help take care of such a creature,
And accommodate her young life to his.
That was what marrying father meant to her.
She had to lie and hear love things made dreadful
By his shouts in the night. He'd shout and shout
Until the strength was shouted out of him,
And his voice died down slowly from exhaustion.
He'd pull his bars apart like bow and bowstring,
And let them go and make them twang, until
His hands had worn them smooth as any oxbow.
And then he'd crow as if he thought that child's play –
The only fun he had. I've heard them say, though,
They found a way to put a stop to it.
He was before my time – I never saw him;
But the pen stayed exactly as it was,
There in the upper chamber in the ell,
A sort of catchall full of attic clutter.
I often think of the smooth hickory bars.
It got so I would say – you know, half fooling –
'It's time I took my turn upstairs in jail' –
Just as you will till it becomes a habit.
No wonder I was glad to get away.
Mind you, I waited till Len said the word.
I didn't want the blame if things went wrong.
I was glad though, no end, when we moved out,
And I looked to be happy, and I was,
As I said, for a while – but I don't know!
Somehow the change wore out like a prescription.

And there's more to it than just window views
And living by a lake. I'm past such help –
Unless Len took the notion, which he won't,
And I won't ask him – it's not sure enough.
I s'pose I've got to go the road I'm going:
Other folks have to, and why shouldn't I?
I almost think if I could do like you,
Drop everything and live out on the ground –
But it might be, come night, I shouldn't like it,
Or a long rain. I should soon get enough,
And be glad of a good roof overhead.
I've lain awake thinking of you, I'll warrant,
More than you have yourself, some of these nights.
The wonder was the tents weren't snatched away
From over you as you lay in your beds.
I haven't courage for a risk like that.
Bless you, of course you're keeping me from work,
But the thing of it is, I need to *be* kept.
There's work enough to do – there's always that;
But behind's behind. The worst that you can do
Is set me back a little more behind.
I shan't catch up in this world, anyway.
I'd *rather* you'd not go unless you must.

AFTER APPLE-PICKING

My long two-pointed ladder's sticking through a tree
Toward heaven still,
And there's a barrel that I didn't fill
Beside it, and there may be two or three
Apples I didn't pick upon some bough.
But I am done with apple-picking now.
Essence of winter sleep is on the night,
The scent of apples: I am drowsing off.

I cannot rub the strangeness from my sight
I got from looking through a pane of glass
I skimmed this morning from the drinking trough
And held against the world of hoary grass.
It melted, and I let it fall and break.
But I was well
Upon my way to sleep before it fell,
And I could tell
What form my dreaming was about to take.
Magnified apples appear and disappear,
Stem end and blossom end,
And every fleck of russet showing clear.
My instep arch not only keeps the ache,
It keeps the pressure of a ladder-round.
I feel the ladder sway as the boughs bend.
And I keep hearing from the cellar bin
The rumbling sound
Of load on load of apples coming in.
For I have had too much
Of apple-picking: I am overtired
Of the great harvest I myself desired.
There were ten thousand thousand fruit to touch,
Cherish in hand, lift down, and not let fall.
For all
That struck the earth,
No matter if not bruised or spiked with stubble,
Went surely to the cider-apple heap
As of no worth.
One can see what will trouble
This sleep of mine, whatever sleep it is.
Were he not gone,
The woodchuck could say whether it's like his
Long sleep, as I describe its coming on,
Or just some human sleep.

THE FEAR

A lantern-light from deeper in the barn
Shone on a man and woman in the door
And threw their lurching shadows on a house
Nearby, all dark in every glossy window.
A horse's hoof pawed once the hollow floor,
And the back of the gig they stood beside
Moved in a little. The man grasped a wheel.
The woman spoke out sharply, 'Whoa, stand still! –
I saw it just as plain as a white plate,'
She said, 'as the light on the dashboard ran
Along the bushes at the roadside – a man's face.
You *must* have seen it too.'

'I didn't see it.

Are you sure—'

'Yes, I'm sure!'

'– it was a face?'

'Joel, I'll have to look. I can't go in,
I can't, and leave a thing like that unsettled.
Doors locked and curtains drawn will make no difference.
I always have felt strange when we came home
To the dark house after so long an absence,
And the key rattled loudly into place
Seemed to warn someone to be getting out
At one door as we entered at another.
What if I'm right, and someone all the time –
Don't hold my arm!'

'I say it's someone passing.'

'You speak as if this were a traveled road.
You forget where we are. What is beyond
That he'd be going to or coming from

At such an hour of night, and on foot too?
What was he standing still for in the bushes?'

'It's not so very late – it's only dark.
There's more in it than you're inclined to say.
Did he look like —?'

'He looked like anyone.
I'll never rest tonight unless I know.
Give me the lantern.'

'You don't want the lantern.'

She pushed past him and got it for herself.

'You're not to come,' she said. 'This is my business.
If the time's come to face it, I'm the one
To put it the right way. He'd never dare –
Listen! He kicked a stone. Hear that, hear that!
He's coming towards us. Joel, *go* in – please.
Hark! – I don't hear him now. But please go in.'

'In the first place you can't make me believe it's —'

'It is – or someone else he's sent to watch.
And now's the time to have it out with him
While we know definitely where he is.
Let him get off and he'll be everywhere
Around us, looking out of trees and bushes
Till I shan't dare to set a foot outdoors.
And I can't stand it. Joel, let me go!'

'But it's nonsense to think he'd care enough.'

'You mean you couldn't understand his caring.
Oh, but you see he hadn't had enough –
Joel, I won't – I won't – I promise you.
We mustn't say hard things. You mustn't either.'

'I'll be the one, if anybody goes!
But you give him the advantage with this light.

What couldn't he do to us standing here!
And if to see was what he wanted, why,
He has seen all there was to see and gone.'

He appeared to forget to keep his hold,
But advanced with her as she crossed the grass.

'What do you want?' she cried to all the dark.
She stretched up tall to overlook the light
That hung in both hands, hot against her skirt.

'There's no one; so you're wrong,' he said.

'There is. –
What do you want?' she cried, and then herself
Was startled when an answer really came.

'Nothing.' It came from well along the road.

She reached a hand to Joel for support:
The smell of scorching woolen made her faint.
'What are you doing round this house at night?'

'Nothing.' A pause: there seemed no more to say.

And then the voice again: 'You seem afraid.
I saw by the way you whipped up the horse.
I'll just come forward in the lantern-light
And let you see.'

'Yes, do. – Joel, go back!'

She stood her ground against the noisy steps
That came on, but her body rocked a little.

'You see,' the voice said.

'Oh.' She looked and looked.

'You don't see – I've a child here by the hand.
A robber wouldn't have his family with him.'

'What's a child doing at this time of night —?'

'Out walking. Every child should have the memory
Of at least one long-after-bedtime walk.
What, son?'
'Then I should think you'd try to find
Somewhere to walk —'
'The highway, as it happens –
We're stopping for the fortnight down at Dean's.'

'But if that's all – Joel – you realize –
You won't think anything. You understand?
You understand that we have to be careful.
This is a very, very lonely place. –
Joel!' She spoke as if she couldn't turn.
The swinging lantern lengthened to the ground,
It touched, it struck, it clattered and went out.

THE WOOD-PILE

Out walking in the frozen swamp one gray day,
I paused and said, 'I will turn back from here.
No, I will go on farther – and we shall see.'
The hard snow held me, save where now and then
One foot went through. The view was all in lines
Straight up and down of tall slim trees
Too much alike to mark or name a place by
So as to say for certain I was here
Or somewhere else: I was just far from home.
A small bird flew before me. He was careful
To put a tree between us when he lighted,
And say no word to tell me who he was
Who was so foolish as to think what *he* thought.
He thought that I was after him for a feather –
The white one in his tail; like one who takes
Everything said as personal to himself.

One flight out sideways would have undeceived him.
And then there was a pile of wood for which
I forgot him and let his little fear
Carry him off the way I might have gone,
Without so much as wishing him good-night.
He went behind it to make his last stand.
It was a cord of maple, cut and split
And piled – and measured, four by four by eight.
And not another like it could I see.
No runner tracks in this year's snow looped near it.
And it was older sure than this year's cutting,
Or even last year's or the year's before.
The wood was gray and the bark warping off it
And the pile somewhat sunken. Clematis
Had wound strings round and round it like a bundle.
What held it, though, on one side was a tree
Still growing, and on one a stake and prop,
These latter about to fall. I thought that only
Someone who lived in turning to fresh tasks
Could so forget his handiwork on which
He spent himself, the labor of his ax,
And leave it there far from a useful fireplace
To warm the frozen swamp as best it could
With the slow smokeless burning of decay.

MOUNTAIN INTERVAL
1916

THE ROAD NOT TAKEN

Two roads diverged in a yellow wood,
And sorry I could not travel both
And be one traveler, long I stood
And looked down one as far as I could
To where it bent in the undergrowth;

Then took the other, as just as fair,
And having perhaps the better claim,
Because it was grassy and wanted wear;
Though as for that, the passing there
Had worn them really about the same,

And both that morning equally lay
In leaves no step had trodden black.
Oh, I kept the first for another day!
Yet knowing how way leads on to way,
I doubted if I should ever come back.

I shall be telling this with a sigh
Somewhere ages and ages hence:
Two roads diverged in a wood, and I –
I took the one less traveled by,
And that has made all the difference.

AN OLD MAN'S WINTER NIGHT

All out-of-doors looked darkly in at him
Through the thin frost, almost in separate stars,
That gathers on the pane in empty rooms.
What kept his eyes from giving back the gaze
Was the lamp tilted near them in his hand.

What kept him from remembering what it was
That brought him to that creaking room was age.
He stood with barrels round him – at a loss.
And having scared the cellar under him
In clomping here, he scared it once again
In clomping off – and scared the outer night,
Which has its sounds, familiar, like the roar
Of trees and crack of branches, common things,
But nothing so like beating on a box.
A light he was to no one but himself.
Where now he sat, concerned with he knew what,
A quiet light, and then not even that.
He consigned to the moon – such as she was,
So late-arising – to the broken moon,
As better than the sun in any case
For such a charge, his snow upon the roof,
His icicles along the wall to keep;
And slept. The log that shifted with a jolt
Once in the stove, disturbed him and he shifted,
And eased his heavy breathing, but still slept.
One aged man – one man – can't keep a house,
A farm, a countryside, or if he can,
It's thus he does it of a winter night.

THE EXPOSED NEST

You were forever finding some new play.
So when I saw you down on hands and knees
In the meadow, busy with the new-cut hay,
Trying, I thought, to set it up on end,
I went to show you how to make it stay,
If that was your idea, against the breeze,
And, if you asked me, even help pretend
To make it root again and grow afresh.

But 'twas no make-believe with you today,
Nor was the grass itself your real concern,
Though I found your hand full of wilted fern,
Steel-bright June-grass, and blackening heads of clover.
'Twas a nest full of young birds on the ground
The cutter bar had just gone champing over
(Miraculously without tasting flesh)
And left defenseless to the heat and light.
You wanted to restore them to their right
Of something interposed between their sight
And too much world at once – could means be found.
The way the nest-full every time we stirred
Stood up to us as to a mother-bird
Whose coming home has been too long deferred,
Made me ask would the mother-bird return
And care for them in such a change of scene,
And might our meddling make her more afraid.
That was a thing we could not wait to learn.
We saw the risk we took in doing good,
But dared not spare to do the best we could
Though harm should come of it; so built the screen
You had begun, and gave them back their shade.
All this to prove we cared. Why is there then
No more to tell? We turned to other things.
I haven't any memory – have you? –
Of ever coming to the place again
To see if the birds lived the first night through,
And so at last to learn to use their wings.

MEETING AND PASSING

As I went down the hill along the wall
There was a gate I had leaned at for the view
And had just turned from when I first saw you

As you came up the hill. We met. But all
We did that day was mingle great and small
Footprints in summer dust as if we drew
The figure of our being less than two
But more than one as yet. Your parasol
Pointed the decimal off with one deep thrust.
And all the time we talked you seemed to see
Something down there to smile at in the dust.
(Oh, it was without prejudice to me!)
Afterward I went past what you had passed
Before we met, and you what I had passed.

THE OVEN BIRD

There is a singer everyone has heard,
Loud, a mid-summer and a mid-wood bird,
Who makes the solid tree trunks sound again.
He says that leaves are old and that for flowers
Mid-summer is to spring as one to ten.
He says the early petal-fall is past,
When pear and cherry bloom went down in showers
On sunny days a moment overcast;
And comes that other fall we name the fall.
He says the highway dust is over all.
The bird would cease and be as other birds
But that he knows in singing not to sing.
The question that he frames in all but words
Is what to make of a diminished thing.

BIRCHES

When I see birches bend to left and right
Across the lines of straighter darker trees,

I like to think some boy's been swinging them.
But swinging doesn't bend them down to stay
As ice storms do. Often you must have seen them
Loaded with ice a sunny winter morning
After a rain. They click upon themselves
As the breeze rises, and turn many-colored
As the stir cracks and crazes their enamel.
Soon the sun's warmth makes them shed crystal shells
Shattering and avalanching on the snow crust –
Such heaps of broken glass to sweep away
You'd think the inner dome of heaven had fallen.
They are dragged to the withered bracken by the load,
And they seem not to break; though once they are bowed
So low for long, they never right themselves:
You may see their trunks arching in the woods
Years afterwards, trailing their leaves on the ground
Like girls on hands and knees that throw their hair
Before them over their heads to dry in the sun.
But I was going to say when Truth broke in
With all her matter of fact about the ice storm,
I should prefer to have some boy bend them
As he went out and in to fetch the cows –
Some boy too far from town to learn baseball,
Whose only play was what he found himself,
Summer or winter, and could play alone.
One by one he subdued his father's trees
By riding them down over and over again
Until he took the stiffness out of them,
And not one but hung limp, not one was left
For him to conquer. He learned all there was
To learn about not launching out too soon
And so not carrying the tree away
Clear to the ground. He always kept his poise
To the top branches, climbing carefully
With the same pains you use to fill a cup

Up to the brim, and even above the brim.
Then he flung outward, feet first, with a swish,
Kicking his way down through the air to the ground.
So was I once myself a swinger of birches.
And so I dream of going back to be.
It's when I'm weary of considerations,
And life is too much like a pathless wood
Where your face burns and tickles with the cobwebs
Broken across it, and one eye is weeping
From a twig's having lashed across it open.
I'd like to get away from earth awhile
And then come back to it and begin over.
May no fate willfully misunderstand me
And half grant what I wish and snatch me away
Not to return. Earth's the right place for love:
I don't know where it's likely to go better.
I'd like to go by climbing a birch tree,
And climb black branches up a snow-white trunk
Toward heaven, till the tree could bear no more,
But dipped its top and set me down again.
That would be good both going and coming back.
One could do worse than be a swinger of birches.

PEA BRUSH

I walked down alone Sunday after church
  To the place where John has been cutting trees,
To see for myself about the birch
  He said I could have to bush my peas.

The sun in the new-cut narrow gap
  Was hot enough for the first of May,
And stifling hot with the odor of sap
  From stumps still bleeding their life away.

The frogs that were peeping a thousand shrill
  Wherever the ground was low and wet,
The minute they heard my step went still
  To watch me and see what I came to get.

Birch boughs enough piled everywhere! –
  All fresh and sound from the recent ax.
Time someone came with cart and pair
  And got them off the wild flowers' backs.

They might be good for garden things
  To curl a little finger round,
The same as you seize cat's-cradle strings,
  And lift themselves up off the ground.

Small good to anything growing wild,
  They were crooking many a trillium
That had budded before the boughs were piled
  And since it was coming up had to come.

A TIME TO TALK

When a friend calls to me from the road
And slows his horse to a meaning walk,
I don't stand still and look around
On all the hills I haven't hoed,
And shout from where I am, 'What is it?'
No, not as there is a time to talk.
I thrust my hoe in the mellow ground,
Blade-end up and five feet tall,
And plod: I go up to the stone wall
For a friendly visit.

THE COW IN APPLE TIME

Something inspires the only cow of late
To make no more of a wall than an open gate,
And think no more of wall-builders than fools.
Her face is flecked with pomace and she drools
A cider syrup. Having tasted fruit,
She scorns a pasture withering to the root.
She runs from tree to tree where lie and sweeten
The windfalls spiked with stubble and worm-eaten.
She leaves them bitten when she has to fly.
She bellows on a knoll against the sky.
Her udder shrivels and the milk goes dry.

AN ENCOUNTER

Once on the kind of day called 'weather breeder,'
When the heat slowly hazes and the sun
By its own power seems to be undone,
I was half boring through, half climbing through
A swamp of cedar. Choked with oil of cedar
And scurf of plants, and weary and overheated,
And sorry I ever left the road I knew,
I paused and rested on a sort of hook
That had me by the coat as good as seated,
And since there was no other way to look,
Looked up toward heaven, and there against the blue,
Stood over me a resurrected tree,
A tree that had been down and raised again –
A barkless specter. He had halted too,
As if for fear of treading upon me.
I saw the strange position of his hands –
Up at his shoulders, dragging yellow strands
Of wire with something in it from men to men.

'You here?' I said. 'Where aren't you nowadays?
And what's the news you carry – if you know?
And tell me where you're off for – Montreal?
Me? I'm not off for anywhere at all.
Sometimes I wander out of beaten ways
Half looking for the orchid Calypso.'

RANGE-FINDING

The battle rent a cobweb diamond-strung
And cut a flower beside a groundbird's nest
Before it stained a single human breast.
The stricken flower bent double and so hung.
And still the bird revisited her young.
A butterfly its fall had dispossessed,
A moment sought in air his flower of rest,
Then lightly stooped to it and fluttering clung.
On the bare upland pasture there had spread
O'ernight 'twixt mullein stalks a wheel of thread
And straining cables wet with silver dew.
A sudden passing bullet shook it dry.
The indwelling spider ran to greet the fly.
But finding nothing, sullenly withdrew.

THE HILL WIFE

I. LONELINESS

Her Word

One ought not to have to care
  So much as you and I
Care when the birds come round the house
  To seem to say good-by;

Or care so much when they come back
  With whatever it is they sing;
The truth being we are as much
  Too glad for the one thing

As we are too sad for the other here –
  With birds that fill their breasts
But with each other and themselves
  And their built or driven nests.

II. HOUSE FEAR

Always – I tell you this they learned –
Always at night when they returned
To the lonely house from far away,
To lamps unlighted and fire gone gray,
They learned to rattle the lock and key
To give whatever might chance to be,
Warning and time to be off in flight:
And preferring the out- to the indoor night,
They learned to leave the house door wide
Until they had lit the lamp inside.

III. THE SMILE

Her Word

I didn't like the way he went away.
That smile! It never came of being gay.
Still he smiled – did you see him? – I was sure!
Perhaps because we gave him only bread
And the wretch knew from that that we were poor.
Perhaps because he let us give instead
Of seizing from us as he might have seized.
Perhaps he mocked at us for being wed,
Or being very young (and he was pleased
To have a vision of us old and dead).
I wonder how far down the road he's got.
He's watching from the woods as like as not.

IV. THE OFT-REPEATED DREAM

She had no saying dark enough
  For the dark pine that kept
Forever trying the window latch
  Of the room where they slept.

The tireless but ineffectual hands
  That with every futile pass
Made the great tree seem as a little bird
  Before the mystery of glass!

It never had been inside the room,
  And only one of the two
Was afraid in an oft-repeated dream
  Of what the tree might do.

V. THE IMPULSE

It was too lonely for her there,
  And too wild,
And since there were but two of them,
  And no child,

And work was little in the house,
  She was free,
And followed where he furrowed field,
  Or felled tree.

She rested on a log and tossed
  The fresh chips,
With a song only to herself
  On her lips.

And once she went to break a bough
  Of black alder.
She strayed so far she scarcely heard
  When he called her –

And didn't answer – didn't speak –
  Or return.
She stood, and then she ran and hid
  In the fern.

He never found her, though he looked
  Everywhere,
And he asked at her mother's house
  Was she there.

Sudden and swift and light as that
  The ties gave,
And he learned of finalities
  Besides the grave.

LOCKED OUT

As told to a child

When we locked up the house at night,
We always locked the flowers outside
And cut them off from window light.
The time I dreamed the door was tried
And brushed with buttons upon sleeves,
The flowers were out there with the thieves.
Yet nobody molested them!
We did find one nasturtium
Upon the steps with bitten stem.
I may have been to blame for that:
I always thought it must have been
Some flower I played with as I sat
At dusk to watch the moon down early.

'OUT, OUT –'

The buzz saw snarled and rattled in the yard
And made dust and dropped stove-length sticks of wood,
Sweet-scented stuff when the breeze drew across it.
And from there those that lifted eyes could count
Five mountain ranges one behind the other
Under the sunset far into Vermont.
And the saw snarled and rattled, snarled and rattled,
As it ran light, or had to bear a load.
And nothing happened: day was all but done.
Call it a day, I wish they might have said
To please the boy by giving him the half hour
That a boy counts so much when saved from work.
His sister stood beside them in her apron
To tell them 'Supper.' At the word, the saw,
As if to prove saws knew what supper meant,

Leaped out at the boy's hand, or seemed to leap –
He must have given the hand. However it was,
Neither refused the meeting. But the hand!
The boy's first outcry was a rueful laugh,
As he swung toward them holding up the hand,
Half in appeal, but half as if to keep
The life from spilling. Then the boy saw all –
Since he was old enough to know, big boy
Doing a man's work, though a child at heart –
He saw all spoiled. 'Don't let him cut my hand off –
The doctor, when he comes. Don't let him, sister!'
So. But the hand was gone already.
The doctor put him in the dark of ether.
He lay and puffed his lips out with his breath.
And then – the watcher at his pulse took fright.
No one believed. They listened at his heart.
Little – less – nothing! – and that ended it.
No more to build on there. And they, since they
Were not the one dead, turned to their affairs.

THE GUM-GATHERER

There overtook me and drew me in
To his downhill, early-morning stride,
And set me five miles on my road
Better than if he had had me ride,
A man with a swinging bag for load
And half the bag wound round his hand.
We talked like barking above the din
Of water we walked along beside.
And for my telling him where I'd been
And where I lived in mountain land
To be coming home the way I was,
He told me a little about himself.

He came from higher up in the pass
Where the grist of the new-beginning brooks
Is blocks split off the mountain mass –
And hopeless grist enough it looks
Ever to grind to soil for grass.
(The way it is will do for moss.)
There he had built his stolen shack.
It had to be a stolen shack
Because of the fears of fire and loss
That trouble the sleep of lumber folk:
Visions of half the world burned black
And the sun shrunken yellow in smoke.
We know who when they come to town
Bring berries under the wagon seat,
Or a basket of eggs between their feet;
What this man brought in a cotton sack
Was gum, the gum of the mountain spruce.
He showed me lumps of the scented stuff
Like uncut jewels, dull and rough.
It comes to market golden brown;
But turns to pink between the teeth.

I told him this is a pleasant life,
To set your breast to the bark of trees
That all your days are dim beneath,
And reaching up with a little knife,
To loose the resin and take it down
And bring it to market when you please.

SNOW

The three stood listening to a fresh access
Of wind that caught against the house a moment,
Gulped snow, and then blew free again – the Coles,

Dressed, but disheveled from some hours of sleep;
Meserve, belittled in the great skin coat he wore.

Meserve was first to speak. He pointed backward
Over his shoulder with his pipestem, saying,
'You can just see it glancing off the roof
Making a great scroll upward toward the sky,
Long enough for recording all our names on. –
I think I'll just call up my wife and tell her
I'm here – so far – and starting on again.
I'll call her softly so that if she's wise
And gone to sleep, she needn't wake to answer.'
Three times he barely stirred the bell, then listened.
'Why, Lett, still up? Lett, I'm at Cole's. I'm late.
I called you up to say Good-night from here
Before I went to say Good-morning there. –
I thought I would. – I know, but, Lett – I know –
I could, but what's the sense? The rest won't be
So bad. – Give me an hour for it. – Ho, ho,
Three hours to here! But that was all uphill;
The rest is down. – Why no, no, not a wallow:
They kept their heads and took their time to it
Like darlings, both of them. They're in the barn. –
My dear, I'm coming just the same. I didn't
Call you to ask you to invite me home. –'
He lingered for some word she wouldn't say,
Said it at last himself, 'Good-night,' and then,
Getting no answer, closed the telephone.
The three stood in the lamplight round the table
With lowered eyes a moment till he said,
'I'll just see how the horses are.'

'Yes, do,'
Both the Coles said together. Mrs Cole
Added: 'You can judge better after seeing. –
I want you here with me, Fred. – Leave him here,

Brother Meserve. You know to find your way
Out through the shed.'

'I guess I know my way.
I guess I know where I can find my name
Carved in the shed to tell me who I am
If it don't tell me where I am. I used
To play —'

'You tend your horses and come back. –
Fred Cole, you're going to let him!'

'Well, aren't you?
How can you help yourself?'

'I called him Brother.
Why did I call him that?'

'It's right enough.
That's all you ever heard him called round here.
He seems to have lost off his Christian name.'

'Christian enough I should call that myself.
He took no notice, did he? Well, at least
I didn't use it out of love of him,
The dear knows. I detest the thought of him –
With his ten children under ten years old.
I hate his wretched little Racker Sect,
All's ever I heard of it, which isn't much.
But that's not saying – look, Fred Cole, it's twelve,
Isn't it, now? He's been here half an hour.
He says he left the village store at nine:
Three hours to do four miles – a mile an hour
Or not much better. Why, it doesn't seem
As if a man could move that slow and move.

Try to think what he did with all that time.
And three miles more to go!'

'Don't let him go.
Stick to him, Helen. Make him answer you.
That sort of man talks straight-on all his life
From the last thing he said himself, stone deaf
To anything anyone else may say.
I should have thought, though, you could make him hear you.'

'What is he doing out a night like this?
Why can't he stay at home?'

'He had to preach.'

'It's no night to be out.'

'He may be small,
He may be good, but one thing's sure, he's tough.'

'And strong of stale tobacco.'

'He'll pull through.'

'You only say so. Not another house
Or shelter to put into from this place
To theirs. I'm going to call his wife again.'

'Wait and he may. Let's see what he will do.
Let's see if he will think of her again.
But then, I doubt he's thinking of himself.
He doesn't look on it as anything.'

'He shan't go – there!'

'It *is* a night, my dear.'

'One thing: he didn't drag God into it.'

'He don't consider it a case for God.'

'You think so, do you? You don't know the kind.
He's getting up a miracle this minute.
Privately – to himself, right now, he's thinking
He'll make a case of it if he succeeds,
But keep still if he fails.'

'Keep still all over.
He'll be dead – dead and buried.'

'Such a trouble!
Not but I've every reason not to care
What happens to him if it only takes
Some of the sanctimonious conceit
Out of one of those pious scalawags.'

'Nonsense to that! You want to see him safe.'

'You like the runt.'

'Don't you a little?'

'Well,
I don't like what he's doing, which is what
You like, and like him for.'

'Oh, yes you do.
You like your fun as well as anyone;
Only you women have to put these airs on
To impress men. You've got us so ashamed
Of being men we can't look at a good fight
Between two boys and not feel bound to stop it.
Let the man freeze an ear or two, I say. –
He's here. I leave him all to you. Go in
And save his life. – All right, come in, Meserve.
Sit down, sit down. How did you find the horses?'

'Fine, fine.'

'And ready for some more? My wife here
Says it won't do. You've got to give it up.'

'Won't you to please me? Please! If I say Please?
Mr Meserve, I'll leave it to *your* wife.
What *did* your wife say on the telephone?'

Meserve seemed to heed nothing but the lamp
Or something not far from it on the table.

By straightening out and lifting a forefinger,
He pointed with his hand from where it lay
Like a white crumpled spider on his knee:
'That leaf there in your open book! It moved
Just then, I thought. It's stood erect like that,
There on the table, ever since I came,
Trying to turn itself backward or forward,
I've had my eye on it to make out which:
If forward, then it's with a friend's impatience –
You see I know – to get you on to things
It wants to see how you will take; if backward,
It's from regret for something you have passed
And failed to see the good of. Never mind,
Things must expect to come in front of us
A many times – I don't say just how many –
That varies with the things – before we see them.
One of the lies would make it out that nothing
Ever presents itself before us twice.
Where would we be at last if that were so?
Our very life depends on everything's
Recurring till we answer from within.
The thousandth time may prove the charm. – That leaf!
It can't turn either way. It needs the wind's help.
But the wind didn't move it if it moved.
It moved itself. The wind's at naught in here.
It couldn't stir so sensitively poised
A thing as that. It couldn't reach the lamp
To get a puff of black smoke from the flame,
Or blow a rumple in the collie's coat.
You make a little foursquare block of air,
Quiet and light and warm, in spite of all
The illimitable dark and cold and storm,
And by so doing give these three, lamp, dog,
And book-leaf, that keep near you, their repose;
Though for all anyone can tell, repose

May be the thing you haven't, yet you give it.
So false it is that what we haven't we can't give;
So false, that what we always say is true.
I'll have to turn the leaf if no one else will.
It won't lie down. Then let it stand. Who cares?'

'I shouldn't want to hurry you, Meserve,
But if you're going – say you'll stay, you know.
But let me raise this curtain on a scene,
And show you how it's piling up against you.
You see the snow-white through the white of frost?
Ask Helen how far up the sash it's climbed
Since last we read the gauge.'

'It looks as if
Some pallid thing had squashed its features flat
And its eyes shut with overeagerness
To see what people found so interesting
In one another, and had gone to sleep
Of its own stupid lack of understanding,
Or broken its white neck of mushroom stuff
Short off, and died against the windowpane.'

'Brother Meserve, take care, you'll scare yourself
More than you will us with such nightmare talk.
It's you it matters to, because it's you
Who have to go out into it alone.'

'Let him talk, Helen, and perhaps he'll stay.'

'Before you drop the curtain – I'm reminded:
You recollect the boy who came out here
To breathe the air one winter – had a room
Down at the Averys'? Well, one sunny morning
After a downy storm, he passed our place
And found me banking up the house with snow.
And I was burrowing in deep for warmth,
Piling it well above the windowsills.

The snow against the window caught his eye.
"Hey, that's a pretty thought" – those were his words –
"So you can think it's six feet deep outside,
While you sit warm and read up balanced rations.
You can't get too much winter in the winter."
Those were his words. And he went home and all
But banked the daylight out of Avery's windows.
Now you and I would go to no such length.
At the same time you can't deny it makes
It not a mite worse, sitting here, we three,
Playing our fancy, to have the snow-line run
So high across the pane outside. There where
There is a sort of tunnel in the frost –
More like a tunnel than a hole – way down
At the far end of it you see a stir
And quiver like the frayed edge of the drift
Blown in the wind. I *like* that – I like *that*.
Well, now I leave you, people.'

'Come, Meserve,
We thought you were deciding not to go –
The ways you found to say the praise of comfort
And being where you are. You want to stay.'

'I'll own it's cold for such a fall of snow.
This house is frozen brittle, all except
This room you sit in. If you think the wind
Sounds further off, it's not because it's dying;
You're further under in the snow – that's all –
And feel it less. Hear the soft bombs of dust
It bursts against us at the chimney mouth,
And at the eaves. I like it from inside
More than I shall out in it. But the horses
Are rested and it's time to say Good-night,
And let you get to bed again. Good-night,
Sorry I had to break in on your sleep.'

'Lucky for you you did. Lucky for you
You had us for a halfway station
To stop at. If you were the kind of man
Paid heed to women, you'd take my advice
And for your family's sake stay where you are.
But what good is my saying it over and over?
You've done more than you had a right to think
You could do – *now*. You know the risk you take
In going on.'

'Our snowstorms as a rule
Aren't looked on as man-killers, and although
I'd rather be the beast that sleeps the sleep
Under it all, his door sealed up and lost,
Than the man fighting it to keep above it,
Yet think of the small birds at roost and not
In nests. Shall I be counted less than they are?
Their bulk in water would be frozen rock
In no time out tonight. And yet tomorrow
They will come budding boughs from tree to tree,
Flirting their wings and saying Chickadee,
As if not knowing what you meant by the word storm.'

'But why, when no one wants you to, go on?
Your wife – she doesn't want you to. We don't,
And you yourself don't want to. Who else is there?'

'Save us from being cornered by a woman.
Well, there's –' She told Fred afterward that in
The pause right there, she thought the dreaded word
Was coming, 'God.' But no, he only said,
'Well, there's – the storm. That says I must go on.
That wants me as a war might if it came.
Ask any man.'

He threw her that as something
To last her till he got outside the door.

He had Cole with him to the barn to see him off.
When Cole returned he found his wife still standing
Beside the table, near the open book,
Not reading it.

'Well, what kind of a man
Do you call that?' she said.

'He had the gift
Of words, or is it tongues I ought to say?'

'Was ever such a man for seeing likeness?'

'Or disregarding people's civil questions –
What? We've found out in one hour more about him
Than we had seeing him pass by in the road
A thousand times. If that's the way he preaches!
You didn't think you'd keep him after all.
Oh, I'm not blaming you. He didn't leave you
Much say in the matter, and I'm just as glad
We're not in for a night of him. No sleep
If he had stayed. The least thing set him going.
It's quiet as an empty church without him.'

'But how much better off are we as it is?
We'll have to sit here till we know he's safe.'

'Yes, I suppose you'll want to, but I shouldn't.
He knows what he can do, or he wouldn't try.
Get into bed I say, and get some rest.
He won't come back, and if he telephones,
It won't be for an hour or two.'

'Well then –
We can't be any help by sitting here
And living his fight through with him, I suppose.'

*

Cole had been telephoning in the dark.
Mrs Cole's voice came from an inner room:
'Did she call you or you call her?'

'She me.
You'd better dress: you won't go back to bed.
We must have been asleep: it's three and after.'

'Had she been ringing long? I'll get my wrapper.
I want to speak to her.'

'All she said was,
He hadn't come and had he really started.'

'She knew he had, poor thing, two hours ago.'

'He had the shovel. He'll have made a fight.'

'Why did I ever let him leave this house!'

'Don't begin that. You did the best you could
To keep him – though perhaps you didn't quite
Conceal a wish to see him show the spunk
To disobey you. Much his wife'll thank you.'

'Fred, after all I said! You shan't make out
That it was any way but what it was.
Did she let on by any word she said
She didn't thank me?'

'When I told her "Gone,"
"Well then," she said, and "Well then" – like a threat.
And then her voice came scraping slow: "Oh, you,
Why did you let him go?"'

'Asked why we let him?
You let me there. I'll ask her why she let him.
She didn't dare to speak when he was here.
Their number's – twenty-one? – The thing won't work.
Someone's receiver's down. The handle stumbles.
The stubborn thing, the way it jars your arm! –
It's theirs. She's dropped it from her hand and gone.'

'Try speaking. Say "Hello!"'

'Hello. Hello.'

'What do you hear?'

'I hear an empty room –
You know – it sounds that way. And yes, I hear –
I think I hear a clock – and windows rattling.
No step, though. If she's there she's sitting down.'

'Shout, she may hear you.'

'Shouting is no good.'

'Keep speaking, then.'

'Hello. Hello. Hello. –
You don't suppose? – she wouldn't go outdoors?'

'I'm half afraid that's just what she might do.'

'And leave the children?'

'Wait and call again.
You can't hear whether she has left the door
Wide open and the wind's blown out the lamp
And the fire's died and the room's dark and cold?'

'One of two things, either she's gone to bed
Or gone outdoors.'

'In which case both are lost.
Do you know what she's like? Have you ever met her?
It's strange she doesn't want to speak to us.'

'Fred, see if you can hear what I hear. Come.'

'A clock maybe.'

'Don't you hear something else?'

'Not talking.'

'No.'

'Why, yes, I hear – what is it?'

'What do you say it is?'

'A baby's crying!

Frantic it sounds, though muffled and far off.
Its mother wouldn't let it cry like that,
Not if she's there.'

'What do you make of it?'

'There's only one thing possible to make,
That is, assuming – that she has gone out.
Of course she hasn't, though.' They both sat down
Helpless. 'There's nothing we can do till morning.'

'Fred, I shan't let you think of going out.'

'Hold on.' The double bell began to chirp.
They started up. Fred took the telephone.
'Hello, Meserve. You're there, then! – and your wife?
Good! Why I asked – she didn't seem to answer. –
He says she went to let him in the barn. –
We're glad. Oh, say no more about it, man.
Drop in and see us when you're passing.'

'Well,
She has him, then, though what she wants him for
I *don't* see.'

'Possibly not for herself.
Maybe she only wants him for the children.'

'The whole to-do seems to have been for nothing.
What spoiled our night was to him just his fun.
What did he come in for? – to talk and visit?
Thought he'd just call to tell us it was snowing.
If he thinks he is going to make our house
A halfway coffee house 'twixt town and nowhere —'

'I thought you'd feel you'd been too much concerned.'

'You think you haven't been concerned yourself.'

'If you mean he was inconsiderate
To rout us out to think for him at midnight

And then take our advice no more than nothing,
Why, I agree with you. But let's forgive him.
We've had a share in one night of his life.
What'll you bet he ever calls again?'

THE SOUND OF TREES

I wonder about the trees.
Why do we wish to bear
Forever the noise of these
More than another noise
So close to our dwelling place?
We suffer them by the day
Till we lose all measure of pace,
And fixity in our joys,
And acquire a listening air.
They are that that talks of going
But never gets away;
And that talks no less for knowing,
As it grows wiser and older,
That now it means to stay.
My feet tug at the floor
And my head sways to my shoulder
Sometimes when I watch trees sway,
From the window or the door.
I shall set forth for somewhere,
I shall make the reckless choice
Some day when they are in voice
And tossing so as to scare
The white clouds over them on.
I shall have less to say,
But I shall be gone.

NEW HAMPSHIRE

1923

THE CENSUS-TAKER

I came an errand one cloud-blowing evening
To a slab-built, black-paper-covered house
Of one room and one window and one door,
The only dwelling in a waste cut over
A hundred square miles round it in the mountains:
And that not dwelt in now by men or women.
(It never had been dwelt in, though, by women,
So what is this I make a sorrow of?)
I came as census-taker to the waste
To count the people in it and found none,
None in the hundred miles, none in the house,
Where I came last with some hope, but not much,
After hours' overlooking from the cliffs
An emptiness flayed to the very stone.
I found no people that dared show themselves,
None not in hiding from the outward eye.
The time was autumn, but how anyone
Could tell the time of year when every tree
That could have dropped a leaf was down itself
And nothing but the stump of it was left
Now bringing out its rings in sugar of pitch;
And every tree up stood a rotting trunk
Without a single leaf to spend on autumn,
Or branch to whistle after what was spent.
Perhaps the wind the more without the help
Of breathing trees said something of the time
Of year or day the way it swung a door
Forever off the latch, as if rude men
Passed in and slammed it shut each one behind him
For the next one to open for himself.
I counted nine I had no right to count

(But this was dreamy unofficial counting)
Before I made the tenth across the threshold.
Where was my supper? Where was anyone's?
No lamp was lit. Nothing was on the table.
The stove was cold – the stove was off the chimney –
And down by one side where it lacked a leg.
The people that had loudly passed the door
Were people to the ear but not the eye.
They were not on the table with their elbows.
They were not sleeping in the shelves of bunks.
I saw no men there and no bones of men there.
I armed myself against such bones as might be
With the pitch-blackened stub of an ax-handle
I picked up off the straw-dust-covered floor.
Not bones, but the ill-fitted window rattled.
The door was still because I held it shut
While I thought what to do that could be done –
About the house – about the people not there.
This house in one year fallen to decay
Filled me with no less sorrow than the houses
Fallen to ruin in ten thousand years
Where Asia wedges Africa from Europe.
Nothing was left to do that I could see
Unless to find that there was no one there
And declare to the cliffs too far for echo,
'The place is desert, and let whoso lurks
In silence, if in this he is aggrieved,
Break silence now or be forever silent.
Let him say why it should not be declared so.'
The melancholy of having to count souls
Where they grow fewer and fewer every year
Is extreme where they shrink to none at all.
It must be I want life to go on living.

THE STAR-SPLITTER

'You know Orion always comes up sideways.
Throwing a leg up over our fence of mountains,
And rising on his hands, he looks in on me
Busy outdoors by lantern-light with something
I should have done by daylight, and indeed,
After the ground is frozen, I should have done
Before it froze, and a gust flings a handful
Of waste leaves at my smoky lantern chimney
To make fun of my way of doing things,
Or else fun of Orion's having caught me.
Has a man, I should like to ask, no rights
These forces are obliged to pay respect to?'
So Brad McLaughlin mingled reckless talk
Of heavenly stars with hugger-mugger farming,
Till having failed at hugger-mugger farming
He burned his house down for the fire insurance
And spent the proceeds on a telescope
To satisfy a lifelong curiosity
About our place among the infinities.

'What do you want with one of those blame things?'
I asked him well beforehand. 'Don't you get one!'

'Don't call it blamed; there isn't anything
More blameless in the sense of being less
A weapon in our human fight,' he said.
'I'll have one if I sell my farm to buy it.'
There where he moved the rocks to plow the ground
And plowed between the rocks he couldn't move,
Few farms changed hands; so rather than spend years
Trying to sell his farm and then not selling,
He burned his house down for the fire insurance
And bought the telescope with what it came to.

He had been heard to say by several:
'The best thing that we're put here for's to see;
The strongest thing that's given us to see with's
A telescope. Someone in every town
Seems to me owes it to the town to keep one.
In Littleton it may as well be me.'
After such loose talk it was no surprise
When he did what he did and burned his house down.

Mean laughter went about the town that day
To let him know we weren't the least imposed on,
And he could wait – we'd see to him tomorrow.
But the first thing next morning we reflected
If one by one we counted people out
For the least sin, it wouldn't take us long
To get so we had no one left to live with.
For to be social is to be forgiving.
Our thief, the one who does our stealing from us,
We don't cut off from coming to church suppers,
But what we miss we go to him and ask for.
He promptly gives it back, that is if still
Uneaten, unworn out, or undisposed of.
It wouldn't do to be too hard on Brad
About his telescope. Beyond the age
Of being given one for Christmas gift,
He had to take the best way he knew how
To find himself in one. Well, all we said was
He took a strange thing to be roguish over.
Some sympathy was wasted on the house,
A good old-timer dating back along;
But a house isn't sentient; the house
Didn't feel anything. And if it did,
Why not regard it as a sacrifice,
And an old-fashioned sacrifice by fire,
Instead of a new-fashioned one at auction?

Out of a house and so out of a farm
At one stroke (of a match), Brad had to turn
To earn a living on the Concord railroad,
As under-ticket-agent at a station
Where his job, when he wasn't selling tickets,
Was setting out, up track and down, not plants
As on a farm, but planets, evening stars
That varied in their hue from red to green.

He got a good glass for six hundred dollars.
His new job gave him leisure for stargazing.
Often he bid me come and have a look
Up the brass barrel, velvet black inside,
At a star quaking in the other end.
I recollect a night of broken clouds
And underfoot snow melted down to ice,
And melting further in the wind to mud.
Bradford and I had out the telescope.
We spread our two legs as we spread its three,
Pointed our thoughts the way we pointed it,
And standing at our leisure till the day broke,
Said some of the best things we ever said.
That telescope was christened the Star-Splitter,
Because it didn't do a thing but split
A star in two or three, the way you split
A globule of quicksilver in your hand
With one stroke of your finger in the middle.
It's a star-splitter if there ever was one,
And ought to do some good if splitting stars
'Sa thing to be compared with splitting wood.

We've looked and looked, but after all where are we?
Do we know any better where we are,
And how it stands between the night tonight
And a man with a smoky lantern chimney?
How different from the way it ever stood?

PAUL'S WIFE

To drive Paul out of any lumber camp
All that was needed was to say to him,
'How is the wife, Paul?' – and he'd disappear.
Some said it was because he had no wife,
And hated to be twitted on the subject;
Others because he'd come within a day
Or so of having one, and then been jilted;
Others because he'd had one once, a good one,
Who'd run away with someone else and left him;
And others still because he had one now
He only had to be reminded of –
He was all duty to her in a minute:
He had to run right off to look her up,
As if to say, 'That's so, how is my wife?
I hope she isn't getting into mischief.'
No one was anxious to get rid of Paul.
He'd been the hero of the mountain camps
Ever since, just to show them, he had slipped
The bark of a whole tamarack off whole,
As clean as boys do off a willow twig
To make a willow whistle on a Sunday
In April by subsiding meadow brooks.
They seemed to ask him just to see him go,
'How is the wife, Paul?' and he always went.
He never stopped to murder anyone
Who asked the question. He just disappeared –
Nobody knew in what direction,
Although it wasn't usually long
Before they heard of him in some new camp,
The same Paul at the same old feats of logging.
The question everywhere was why should Paul
Object to being asked a civil question –
A man you could say almost anything to

Short of a fighting word. You have the answers.
And there was one more not so fair to Paul:
That Paul had married a wife not his equal.
Paul was ashamed of her. To match a hero
She would have had to be a heroine;
Instead of which she was some half-breed squaw.
But if the story Murphy told was true,
She wasn't anything to be ashamed of.

You know Paul could do wonders. Everyone's
Heard how he thrashed the horses on a load
That wouldn't budge, until they simply stretched
Their rawhide harness from the load to camp.
Paul told the boss the load would be all right,
'The sun will bring your load in' – and it did –
By shrinking the rawhide to natural length.
That's what is called a stretcher. But I guess
The one about his jumping so's to land
With both his feet at once against the ceiling,
And then land safely right side up again,
Back on the floor, is fact or pretty near fact.
Well, this is such a yarn. Paul sawed his wife
Out of a white-pine log. Murphy was there
And, as you might say, saw the lady born.
Paul worked at anything in lumbering.
He'd been hard at it taking boards away
For – I forget – the last ambitious sawyer
To want to find out if he couldn't pile
The lumber on Paul till Paul begged for mercy.
They'd sliced the first slab off a big butt log,
And the sawyer had slammed the carriage back
To slam end-on again against the saw teeth.
To judge them by the way they caught themselves
When they saw what had happened to the log,
They must have had a guilty expectation

Something was going to go with their slambanging.
Something had left a broad black streak of grease
On the new wood the whole length of the log
Except, perhaps, a foot at either end.
But when Paul put his finger in the grease,
It wasn't grease at all, but a long slot.
The log was hollow. They were sawing pine.
'First time I ever saw a hollow pine.
That comes of having Paul around the place.
Take it to hell for me,' the sawyer said.
Everyone had to have a look at it,
And tell Paul what he ought to do about it.
(They treated it as his.) 'You take a jackknife,
And spread the opening, and you've got a dugout
All dug to go a-fishing in.' To Paul
The hollow looked too sound and clean and empty
Ever to have housed birds or beasts or bees.
There was no entrance for them to get in by.
It looked to him like some new kind of hollow
He thought he'd *better* take his jackknife to.
So after work that evening he came back
And let enough light into it by cutting
To see if it was empty. He made out in there
A slender length of pith, or was it pith?
It might have been the skin a snake had cast
And left stood up on end inside the tree
The hundred years the tree must have been growing.
More cutting and he had this in both hands,
And looking from it to the pond nearby,
Paul wondered how it would respond to water.
Not a breeze stirred, but just the breath of air
He made in walking slowly to the beach
Blew it once off his hands and almost broke it.
He laid it at the edge, where it could drink.
At the first drink it rustled and grew limp.

At the next drink it grew invisible.
Paul dragged the shallows for it with his fingers,
And thought it must have melted. It was gone.
And then beyond the open water, dim with midges,
Where the log drive lay pressed against the boom,
It slowly rose a person, rose a girl,
Her wet hair heavy on her like a helmet,
Who, leaning on a log, looked back at Paul.
And that made Paul in turn look back
To see if it was anyone behind him
That she was looking at instead of him.
(Murphy had been there watching all the time,
But from a shed where neither of them could see him.)
There was a moment of suspense in birth
When the girl seemed too waterlogged to live,
Before she caught her first breath with a gasp
And laughed. Then she climbed slowly to her feet,
And walked off, talking to herself or Paul,
Across the logs like backs of alligators,
Paul taking after her around the pond.

Next evening Murphy and some other fellows
Got drunk, and tracked the pair up Catamount,
From the bare top of which there is a view
To other hills across a kettle valley.
And there, well after dark, let Murphy tell it,
They saw Paul and his creature keeping house.
It was the only glimpse that anyone
Has had of Paul and her since Murphy saw them
Falling in love across the twilight millpond.
More than a mile across the wilderness
They sat together halfway up a cliff
In a small niche let into it, the girl
Brightly, as if a star played on the place,
Paul darkly, like her shadow. All the light

Was from the girl herself, though, not from a star,
As was apparent from what happened next.
All those great ruffians put their throats together,
And let out a loud yell, and threw a bottle,
As a brute tribute of respect to beauty.
Of course the bottle fell short by a mile,
But the shout reached the girl and put her light out.
She went out like a firefly, and that was all.

So there were witnesses that Paul was married,
And not to anyone to be ashamed of.
Everyone had been wrong in judging Paul.
Murphy told me Paul put on all those airs
About his wife to keep her to himself.
Paul was what's called a terrible possessor.
Owning a wife with him meant owning her.
She wasn't anybody else's business,
Either to praise her or so much as name her,
And he'd thank people not to think of her.
Murphy's idea was that a man like Paul
Wouldn't be spoken to about a wife
In any way the world knew how to speak.

WILD GRAPES

What tree may not the fig be gathered from?
The grape may not be gathered from the birch?
It's all you know the grape, or know the birch.
As a girl gathered from the birch myself
Equally with my weight in grapes, one autumn,
I ought to know what tree the grape is fruit of.
I was born, I suppose, like anyone,
And grew to be a little boyish girl
My brother could not always leave at home.

But that beginning was wiped out in fear
The day I swung suspended with the grapes,
And was come after like Eurydice
And brought down safely from the upper regions;
And the life I live now's an extra life
I can waste as I please on whom I please.
So if you see me celebrate two birthdays,
And give myself out as two different ages,
One of them five years younger than I look –

One day my brother led me to a glade
Where a white birch he knew of stood alone,
Wearing a thin headdress of pointed leaves,
And heavy on her heavy hair behind,
Against her neck, an ornament of grapes.
Grapes, I knew grapes from having seen them last year.
One bunch of them, and there began to be
Bunches all round me growing in white birches,
The way they grew round Leif the Lucky's German;
Mostly as much beyond my lifted hands, though,
As the moon used to seem when I was younger,
And only freely to be had for climbing.
My brother did the climbing; and at first
Threw me down grapes to miss and scatter
And have to hunt for in sweet fern and hardhack;
Which gave him some time to himself to eat,
But not so much, perhaps, as a boy needed.
So then, to make me wholly self-supporting,
He climbed still higher and bent the tree to earth
And put it in my hands to pick my own grapes.
'Here, take a treetop, I'll get down another.
Hold on with all your might when I let go.'
I said I had the tree. It wasn't true.
The opposite was true. The tree had me.
The minute it was left with me alone,

It caught me up as if I were the fish
And it the fishpole. So I was translated,
To loud cries from my brother of 'Let go!
Don't you know anything, you girl? Let go!'
But I, with something of the baby grip
Acquired ancestrally in just such trees
When wilder mothers than our wildest now
Hung babies out on branches by the hands
To dry or wash or tan, I don't know which
(You'll have to ask an evolutionist) –
I held on uncomplainingly for life.
My brother tried to make me laugh to help me.
'What are you doing up there in those grapes?
Don't be afraid. A few of them won't hurt you.
I mean, they won't pick you if you don't them.'
Much danger of my picking anything!
By that time I was pretty well reduced
To a philosophy of hang-and-let-hang.
'Now you know how it feels,' my brother said,
'To be a bunch of fox grapes, as they call them,
That when it thinks it has escaped the fox
By growing where it shouldn't – on a birch,
Where a fox wouldn't think to look for it –
And if he looked and found it, couldn't reach it –
Just then come you and I to gather it.
Only you have the advantage of the grapes
In one way: you have one more stem to cling by,
And promise more resistance to the picker.'

One by one I lost off my hat and shoes,
And still I clung. I let my head fall back,
And shut my eyes against the sun, my ears
Against my brother's nonsense. 'Drop,' he said,
'I'll catch you in my arms. It isn't far.'
(Stated in lengths of him it might not be.)

'Drop or I'll shake the tree and shake you down.'
Grim silence on my part as I sank lower,
My small wrists stretching till they showed the banjo strings.
'Why, if she isn't serious about it!
Hold tight awhile till I think what to do.
I'll bend the tree down and let you down by it.'
I don't know much about the letting down;
But once I felt ground with my stocking feet
And the world came revolving back to me,
I know I looked long at my curled-up fingers,
Before I straightened them and brushed the bark off.
My brother said: 'Don't you weigh anything?
Try to weigh something next time, so you won't
Be run off with by birch trees into space.'

It wasn't my not weighing anything
So much as my not knowing anything –
My brother had been nearer right before.
I had not taken the first step in knowledge;
I had not learned to let go with the hands,
As still I have not learned to with the heart,
And have no wish to with the heart – nor need,
That I can see. The mind – is not the heart.
I may yet live, as I know others live,
To wish in vain to let go with the mind –
Of cares, at night, to sleep; but nothing tells me
That I need learn to let go with the heart.

PLACE FOR A THIRD

Nothing to say to all those marriages!
She had made three herself to three of his.
The score was even for them, three to three.

But come to die she found she cared so much:
She thought of children in a burial row;
Three children in a burial row were sad.
One man's three women in a burial row
Somehow made her impatient with the man.
And so she said to Laban, 'You have done
A good deal right; don't do the last thing wrong.
Don't make me lie with those two other women.'

Laban said, No, he would not make her lie
With anyone but that she had a mind to,
If that was how she felt, of course, he said.
She went her way. But Laban having caught
This glimpse of lingering person in Eliza,
And anxious to make all he could of it
With something he remembered in himself,
Tried to think how he could exceed his promise,
And give good measure to the dead, though thankless.
If that was how she felt, he kept repeating.
His first thought under pressure was a grave
In a new-boughten grave plot by herself,
Under he didn't care how great a stone:
He'd sell a yoke of steers to pay for it.
And weren't there special cemetery flowers,
That, once grief sets to growing, grief may rest:
The flowers will go on with grief awhile,
And no one seem neglecting or neglected?
A prudent grief will not despise such aids.
He thought of evergreen and everlasting.
And then he had a thought worth many of these.
Somewhere must be the grave of the young boy
Who married her for playmate more than helpmate,
And sometimes laughed at what it was between them.
How would she like to sleep her last with him?
Where was his grave? Did Laban know his name?

He found the grave a town or two away,
The headstone cut with *John, Beloved Husband,*
Beside it room reserved; the say a sister's,
A never-married sister's of that husband,
Whether Eliza would be welcome there.
The dead was bound to silence: ask the sister.
So Laban saw the sister, and, saying nothing
Of where Eliza wanted *not* to lie,
And who had thought to lay her with her first love,
Begged simply for the grave. The sister's face
Fell all in wrinkles of responsibility.
She wanted to do right. She'd have to think.
Laban was old and poor, yet seemed to care;
And she was old and poor – but she cared, too.
They sat. She cast one dull, old look at him,
Then turned him out to go on other errands
She said he might attend to in the village,
While she made up her mind how much she cared –
And how much Laban cared – and why he cared.
(She made shrewd eyes to see where he came in.)

She'd looked Eliza up her second time,
A widow at her second husband's grave,
And offered her a home to rest awhile
Before she went the poor man's widow's way,
Housekeeping for the next man out of wedlock.
She and Eliza had been friends through all.
Who was she to judge marriage in a world
Whose Bible's so confused in marriage counsel?
The sister had not come across this Laban;
A decent product of life's ironing-out;
She must not keep him waiting. Time would press
Between the death day and the funeral day.
So when she saw him coming in the street
She hurried her decision to be ready

R.F.–6

To meet him with his answer at the door.
Laban had known about what it would be
From the way she had set her poor old mouth,
To do, as she had put it, what was right.

She gave it through the screen door closed between them:
'No, not with John. There wouldn't be no sense.
Eliza's had too many other men.'

Laban was forced to fall back on his plan
To buy Eliza a plot to lie alone in:
Which gives him for himself a choice of lots
When his time comes to die and settle down.

THE WITCH OF COÖS

I stayed the night for shelter at a farm
Behind the mountain, with a mother and son,
Two old-believers. They did all the talking.

MOTHER. Folks think a witch who has familiar spirits
She could call up to pass a winter evening,
But won't, should be burned at the stake or something.
Summoning spirits isn't 'Button, button,
Who's got the button,' I would have them know.

SON. Mother can make a common table rear
And kick with two legs like an army mule.

MOTHER. And when I've done it, what good have I done?
Rather than tip a table for you, let me
Tell you what Ralle the Sioux Control once told me.
He said the dead had souls, but when I asked him
How could that be – I thought the dead were souls –

He broke my trance. Don't that make you suspicious
That there's something the dead are keeping back?
Yes, there's something the dead are keeping back.

SON. You wouldn't want to tell him what we have
Up attic, mother?

MOTHER. Bones – a skeleton.

SON. But the headboard of mother's bed is pushed
Against the attic door: the door is nailed.
It's harmless. Mother hears it in the night,
Halting perplexed behind the barrier
Of door and headboard. Where it wants to get
Is back into the cellar where it came from.

MOTHER. We'll never let them, will we, son? We'll never!

SON. It left the cellar forty years ago
And carried itself like a pile of dishes
Up one flight from the cellar to the kitchen,
Another from the kitchen to the bedroom,
Another from the bedroom to the attic,
Right past both father and mother, and neither stopped it.
Father had gone upstairs; mother was downstairs.
I was a baby: I don't know where I was.

MOTHER. The only fault my husband found with me –
I went to sleep before I went to bed,
Especially in winter when the bed
Might just as well be ice and the clothes snow.
The night the bones came up the cellar stairs
Toffile had gone to bed alone and left me,
But left an open door to cool the room off
So as to sort of turn me out of it.

I was just coming to myself enough
To wonder where the cold was coming from,
When I heard Toffile upstairs in the bedroom
And thought I heard him downstairs in the cellar.
The board we had laid down to walk dry-shod on
When there was water in the cellar in spring
Struck the hard cellar bottom. And then someone
Began the stairs, two footsteps, for each step,
The way a man with one leg and a crutch,
Or a little child, comes up. It wasn't Toffile:
It wasn't anyone who could be there.
The bulkhead double doors were double-locked
And swollen tight and buried under snow.
The cellar windows were banked up with sawdust
And swollen tight and buried under snow.
It was the bones. I knew them – and good reason.
My first impulse was to get to the knob
And hold the door. But the bones didn't try
The door; they halted helpless on the landing,
Waiting for things to happen in their favor.
The faintest restless rustling ran all through them.
I never could have done the things I did
If the wish hadn't been too strong in me
To see how they were mounted for this walk.
I had a vision of them put together
Not like a man, but like a chandelier.
So suddenly I flung the door wide on him.
A moment he stood balancing with emotion,
And all but lost himself. (A tongue of fire
Flashed out and licked along his upper teeth.
Smoke rolled inside the sockets of his eyes.)
Then he came at me with one hand outstretched,
The way he did in life once; but this time
I struck the hand off brittle on the floor,
And fell back from him on the floor myself.

The finger-pieces slid in all directions.
(Where did I see one of those pieces lately?
Hand me my button box – it must be there.)
I sat up on the floor and shouted, 'Toffile,
It's coming up to you.' It had its choice
Of the door to the cellar or the hall.
It took the hall door for the novelty,
And set off briskly for so slow a thing,
Still going every which way in the joints, though,
So that it looked like lightning or a scribble,
From the slap I had just now given its hand.
I listened till it almost climbed the stairs
From the hall to the only finished bedroom,
Before I got up to do anything;
Then ran and shouted, 'Shut the bedroom door,
Toffile, for my sake!' 'Company?' he said,
'Don't make me get up; I'm too warm in bed.'
So lying forward weakly on the handrail
I pushed myself upstairs, and in the light
(The kitchen had been dark) I had to own
I could see nothing. 'Toffile, I don't see it.
It's with us in the room, though. It's the bones.'
'What bones?' 'The cellar bones – out of the grave.'
That made him throw his bare legs out of bed
And sit up by me and take hold of me.
I wanted to put out the light and see
If I could see it, or else mow the room,
With our arms at the level of our knees,
And bring the chalk-pile down. 'I'll tell you what –
It's looking for another door to try.
The uncommonly deep snow has made him think
Of his old song, "The Wild Colonial Boy,"
He always used to sing along the tote road.
He's after an open door to get outdoors.
Let's trap him with an open door up attic.'

Toffile agreed to that, and sure enough,
Almost the moment he was given an opening,
The steps began to climb the attic stairs.
I heard them. Toffile didn't seem to hear them.
'Quick!' I slammed to the door and held the knob.
'Toffile, get nails.' I made him nail the door shut
And push the headboard of the bed against it.
Then we asked was there anything
Up attic that we'd ever want again.
The attic was less to us than the cellar.
If the bones liked the attic, let them have it.
Let them stay in the attic. When they sometimes
Come down the stairs at night and stand perplexed
Behind the door and headboard of the bed,
Brushing their chalky skull with chalky fingers,
With sounds like the dry rattling of a shutter,
That's what I sit up in the dark to say –
To no one anymore since Toffile died.
Let them stay in the attic since they went there.
I promised Toffile to be cruel to them
For helping them be cruel once to him.

SON. We think they had a grave down in the cellar.

MOTHER. We know they had a grave down in the cellar.

SON. We never could find out whose bones they were.

MOTHER. Yes, we could too, son. Tell the truth for once.
They were a man's his father killed for me.
I mean a man he killed instead of me.
The least I could do was help dig their grave.
We were about it one night in the cellar.
Son knows the story: but 'twas not for him
To tell the truth, suppose the time had come.

Son looks surprised to see me end a lie
We'd kept up all these years between ourselves
So as to have it ready for outsiders.
But tonight I don't care enough to lie –
I don't remember why I ever cared.
Toffile, if he were here, I don't believe
Could tell you why he ever cared himself. . . .

She hadn't found the finger-bone she wanted
Among the buttons poured out in her lap.
I verified the name next morning: Toffile.
The rural letter box said Toffile Lajway.

FIRE AND ICE

Some say the world will end in fire,
Some say in ice.
From what I've tasted of desire
I hold with those who favor fire.
But if it had to perish twice,
I think I know enough of hate
To say that for destruction ice
Is also great
And would suffice.

IN A DISUSED GRAVEYARD

The living come with grassy tread
To read the gravestones on the hill;
The graveyard draws the living still,
But never anymore the dead.

The verses in it say and say:
'The ones who living come today
To read the stones and go away
Tomorrow dead will come to stay.'

So sure of death the marbles rhyme,
Yet can't help marking all the time
How no one dead will seem to come.
What is it men are shrinking from?

It would be easy to be clever
And tell the stones: Men hate to die
And have stopped dying now forever.
I think they would believe the lie.

TO E.T.

I slumbered with your poems on my breast,
Spread open as I dropped them half-read through
Like dove wings on a figure on a tomb,
To see if in a dream they brought of you

I might not have the chance I missed in life
Through some delay, and call you to your face
First soldier, and then poet, and then both,
Who died a soldier-poet of your race.

I meant, you meant, that nothing should remain
Unsaid between us, brother, and this remained –
And one thing more that was not then to say:
The Victory for what it lost and gained.

You went to meet the shell's embrace of fire
On Vimy Ridge; and when you fell that day

The war seemed over more for you than me,
But now for me than you – the other way.

How over, though, for even me who knew
The foe thrust back unsafe beyond the Rhine,
If I was not to speak of it to you
And see you pleased once more with words of mine?

THE RUNAWAY

Once when the snow of the year was beginning to fall,
We stopped by a mountain pasture to say, 'Whose colt?'
A little Morgan had one forefoot on the wall,
The other curled at his breast. He dipped his head
And snorted at us. And then he had to bolt.
We heard the miniature thunder where he fled,
And we saw him, or thought we saw him, dim and gray,
Like a shadow against the curtain of falling flakes.
'I think the little fellow's afraid of the snow.
He isn't winter-broken. It isn't play
With the little fellow at all. He's running away.
I doubt if even his mother could tell him, "Sakes,
It's only weather." He'd think she didn't know!
Where is his mother? He can't be out alone.'
And now he comes again with clatter of stone,
And mounts the wall again with whited eyes
And all his tail that isn't hair up straight.
He shudders his coat as if to throw off flies.
'Whoever it is that leaves him out so late,
When other creatures have gone to stall and bin,
Ought to be told to come and take him in.'

STOPPING BY WOODS ON A SNOWY EVENING

Whose woods these are I think I know.
His house is in the village, though;
He will not see me stopping here
To watch his woods fill up with snow.

My little horse must think it queer
To stop without a farmhouse near
Between the woods and frozen lake
The darkest evening of the year.

He gives his harness bells a shake
To ask if there is some mistake.
The only other sound's the sweep
Of easy wind and downy flake.

The woods are lovely, dark, and deep,
But I have promises to keep,
And miles to go before I sleep,
And miles to go before I sleep.

FOR ONCE, THEN, SOMETHING

Others taunt me with having knelt at well-curbs
Always wrong to the light, so never seeing
Deeper down in the well than where the water
Gives me back in a shining surface picture
Me myself in the summer heaven, godlike,
Looking out of a wreath of fern and cloud puffs.
Once, when trying with chin against a well-curb,
I discerned, as I thought, beyond the picture,
Through the picture, a something white, uncertain,
Something more of the depths – and then I lost it.

Water came to rebuke the too clear water.
One drop fell from a fern, and lo, a ripple
Shook whatever it was lay there at bottom,
Blurred it, blotted it out. What was that whiteness?
Truth? A pebble of quartz? For once, then, something.

THE ONSET

Always the same, when on a fated night
At last the gathered snow lets down as white
As may be in dark woods, and with a song
It shall not make again all winter long
Of hissing on the yet uncovered ground,
I almost stumble looking up and round,
As one who overtaken by the end
Gives up his errand, and lets death descend
Upon him where he is, with nothing done
To evil, no important triumph won,
More than if life had never been begun.

Yet all the precedent is on my side:
I know that winter death has never tried
The earth but it has failed: the snow may heap
In long storms an undrifted four feet deep
As measured against maple, birch, and oak,
It cannot check the peeper's silver croak;
And I shall see the snow all go downhill
In water of a slender April rill
That flashes tail through last year's withered brake
And dead weeds, like a disappearing snake.
Nothing will be left white but here a birch,
And there a clump of houses with a church.

TO EARTHWARD

Love at the lips was touch
As sweet as I could bear;
And once that seemed too much;
I lived on air

That crossed me from sweet things,
The flow of – was it musk
From hidden grapevine springs
Downhill at dusk?

I had the swirl and ache
From sprays of honeysuckle
That when they're gathered shake
Dew on the knuckle.

I craved strong sweets, but those
Seemed strong when I was young;
The petal of the rose
It was that stung.

Now no joy but lacks salt,
That is not dashed with pain
And weariness and fault;
I crave the stain

Of tears, the aftermark
Of almost too much love,
The sweet of bitter bark
And burning clove.

When stiff and sore and scarred
I take away my hand
From leaning on it hard
In grass and sand,

The hurt is not enough:
I long for weight and strength
To feel the earth as rough
To all my length.

GOOD-BY AND KEEP COLD

This saying good-by on the edge of the dark
And the cold to an orchard so young in the bark
Reminds me of all that can happen to harm
An orchard away at the end of the farm
All winter, cut off by a hill from the house.
I don't want it girdled by rabbit and mouse,
I don't want it dreamily nibbled for browse
By deer, and I don't want it budded by grouse.
(If certain it wouldn't be idle to call
I'd summon grouse, rabbit, and deer to the wall
And warn them away with a stick for a gun.)
I don't want it stirred by the heat of the sun.
(We made it secure against being, I hope,
By setting it out on a northerly slope.)
No orchard's the worse for the wintriest storm;
But one thing about it, it mustn't get warm.
'How often already you've had to be told,
Keep cold, young orchard. Good-by and keep cold.
Dread fifty above more than fifty below.'
I have to be gone for a season or so.
My business awhile is with different trees,
Less carefully nurtured, less fruitful than these,
And such as is done to their wood with an ax –
Maples and birches and tamaracks.
I wish I could promise to lie in the night
And think of an orchard's arboreal plight
When slowly (and nobody comes with a light)

Its heart sinks lower under the sod.
But something has to be left to God.

TWO LOOK AT TWO

Love and forgetting might have carried them
A little further up the mountainside
With night so near, but not much further up.
They must have halted soon in any case
With thoughts of the path back, how rough it was
With rock and washout, and unsafe in darkness;
When they were halted by a tumbled wall
With barbed-wire binding. They stood facing this,
Spending what onward impulse they still had
In one last look the way they must not go,
On up the failing path, where, if a stone
Or earthslide moved at night, it moved itself;
No footstep moved it. 'This is all,' they sighed,
'Good-night to woods.' But not so; there was more.
A doe from round a spruce stood looking at them
Across the wall, as near the wall as they.
She saw them in their field, they her in hers.
The difficulty of seeing what stood still,
Like some up-ended boulder split in two,
Was in her clouded eyes: they saw no fear there.
She seemed to think that, two thus, they were safe.
Then, as if they were something that, though strange,
She could not trouble her mind with too long,
She sighed and passed unscared along the wall.
'*This*, then, is all. What more is there to ask?'
But no, not yet. A snort to bid them wait.
A buck from round the spruce stood looking at them
Across the wall, as near the wall as they.
This was an antlered buck of lusty nostril,

Not the same doe come back into her place.
He viewed them quizzically with jerks of head,
As if to ask, 'Why don't you make some motion?
Or give some sign of life? Because you can't.
I doubt if you're as living as you look.'
Thus till he had them almost feeling dared
To stretch a proffering hand – and a spell-breaking.
Then he too passed unscared along the wall.
Two had seen two, whichever side you spoke from.
'This *must* be all.' It was all. Still they stood,
A great wave from it going over them,
As if the earth in one unlooked-for favor
Had made them certain earth returned their love.

NOT TO KEEP

They sent him back to her. The letter came
Saying. . . . And she could have him. And before
She could be sure there was no hidden ill
Under the formal writing, he was there,
Living. They gave him back to her alive –
How else? They are not known to send the dead. –
And not disfigured visibly. His face?
His hands? She had to look, to look and ask,
'What is it, dear?' And she had given all
And still she had all – *they* had – they the lucky!
Wasn't she glad now? Everything seemed won,
And all the rest for them permissible ease.
She had to ask, 'What was it, dear?'

'Enough,
Yet not enough. A bullet through and through,
High in the breast. Nothing but what good care
And medicine and rest, and you a week,

Can cure me of to go again.' The same
Grim giving to do over for them both.
She dared no more than ask him with her eyes
How was it with him for a second trial.
And with his eyes he asked her not to ask.
They had given him back to her, but not to keep.

A BOUNDLESS MOMENT

He halted in the wind, and – what was that
Far in the maples, pale, but not a ghost?
He stood there bringing March against his thought,
And yet too ready to believe the most.

'Oh, that's the Paradise-in-Bloom,' I said;
And truly it was fair enough for flowers
Had we but in us to assume in March
Such white luxuriance of May for ours.

We stood a moment so, in a strange world,
Myself as one his own pretense deceives;
And then I said the truth (and we moved on).
A young beech clinging to its last year's leaves.

GATHERING LEAVES

Spades take up leaves
No better than spoons,
And bags full of leaves
Are light as balloons.

I make a great noise
Of rustling all day

Like rabbit and deer
Running away.

But the mountains I raise
Elude my embrace,
Flowing over my arms
And into my face.

I may load and unload
Again and again
Till I fill the whole shed,
And what have I then?

Next to nothing for weight;
And since they grew duller
From contact with earth,
Next to nothing for color.

Next to nothing for use.
But a crop is a crop,
And who's to say where
The harvest shall stop?

MISGIVING

All crying, 'We will go with you, O Wind!'
The foliage follow him, leaf and stem;
But a sleep oppresses them as they go,
And they end by bidding him stay with them.

Since ever they flung abroad in spring
The leaves had promised themselves this flight,
Who now would fain seek sheltering wall,
Or thicket, or hollow place for the night.

And now they answer his summoning blast
With an ever vaguer and vaguer stir,
Or at utmost a little reluctant whirl
That drops them no further than where they were.

I only hope that when I am free,
As they are free, to go in quest
Of the knowledge beyond the bounds of life
It may not seem better to me to rest.

ON A TREE FALLEN ACROSS THE ROAD

(*To hear us talk*)

The tree the tempest with a crash of wood
Throws down in front of us is not to bar
Our passage to our journey's end for good,
But just to ask us who we think we are

Insisting always on our own way so.
She likes to halt us in our runner tracks,
And make us get down in a foot of snow
Debating what to do without an ax.

And yet she knows obstruction is in vain:
We will not be put off the final goal
We have it hidden in us to attain,
Not though we have to seize earth by the pole

And, tired of aimless circling in one place,
Steer straight off after something into space.

OUR SINGING STRENGTH

It snowed in spring on earth so dry and warm
The flakes could find no landing place to form.
Hordes spent themselves to make it wet and cold,
And still they failed of any lasting hold.
They made no white impression on the black.
They disappeared as if earth sent them back.
Not till from separate flakes they changed at night
To almost strips and tapes of ragged white
Did grass and garden ground confess it snowed,
And all go back to winter but the road.
Next day the scene was piled and puffed and dead.
The grass lay flattened under one great tread.
Borne down until the end almost took root,
The rangey bough anticipated fruit
With snowballs cupped in every opening bud.
The road alone maintained itself in mud,
Whatever its secret was of greater heat
From inward fires or brush of passing feet.

In spring more mortal singers than belong
To any one place cover us with song.
Thrush, bluebird, blackbird, sparrow, and robin throng;
Some to go further north to Hudson's Bay,
Some that have come too far north back away,
Really a very few to build and stay.
Now was seen how these liked belated snow.
The fields had nowhere left for them to go;
They'd soon exhausted all there was in flying;
The trees they'd had enough of with once trying
And setting off their heavy powder load.
They could find nothing open but the road.
So there they let their lives be narrowed in
By thousands the bad weather made akin.

The road became a channel running flocks
Of glossy birds like ripples over rocks.
I drove them underfoot in bits of flight
That kept the ground, almost disputing right
Of way with me from apathy of wing,
A talking twitter all they had to sing.
A few I must have driven to despair
Made quick asides, but having done in air
A whir among white branches great and small,
As in some too much carven marble hall
Where one false wing beat would have brought down all,
Came tamely back in front of me, the Drover,
To suffer the same driven nightmare over.
One such storm in a lifetime couldn't teach them
That back behind pursuit it couldn't reach them;
None flew behind me to be left alone.

Well, something for a snowstorm to have shown
The country's singing strength thus brought together,
That though repressed and moody with the weather
Was nonetheless there ready to be freed
And sing the wild flowers up from root and seed.

THE LOCKLESS DOOR

It went many years,
But at last came a knock,
And I thought of the door
With no lock to lock.

I blew out the light,
I tiptoed the floor,
And raised both hands
In prayer to the door.

But the knock came again.
My window was wide;
I climbed on the sill
And descended outside.

Back over the sill
I bade a 'Come in'
To whatever the knock
At the door may have been.

So at a knock
I emptied my cage
To hide in the world
And alter with age.

THE NEED OF BEING VERSED IN COUNTRY THINGS

The house had gone to bring again
To the midnight sky a sunset glow.
Now the chimney was all of the house that stood,
Like a pistil after the petals go.

The barn opposed across the way,
That would have joined the house in flame
Had it been the will of the wind, was left
To bear forsaken the place's name.

No more it opened with all one end
For teams that came by the stony road
To drum on the floor with scurrying hoofs
And brush the mow with the summer load.

The birds that came to it through the air
At broken windows flew out and in,

Their murmur more like the sigh we sigh
From too much dwelling on what has been.

Yet for them the lilac renewed its leaf,
And the aged elm, though touched with fire;
And the dry pump flung up an awkward arm;
And the fence post carried a strand of wire.

For them there was really nothing sad.
But though they rejoiced in the nest they kept,
One had to be versed in country things
Not to believe the phoebes wept.

WEST-RUNNING BROOK

1928

SPRING POOLS

These pools that, though in forests, still reflect
The total sky almost without defect,
And like the flowers beside them, chill and shiver,
Will like the flowers beside them soon be gone,
And yet not out by any brook or river,
But up by roots to bring dark foliage on.

The trees that have it in their pent-up buds
To darken nature and be summer woods –
Let them think twice before they use their powers
To blot out and drink up and sweep away
These flowery waters and these watery flowers
From snow that melted only yesterday

THE ROSE FAMILY

The rose is a rose,
And was always a rose.
But the theory now goes
That the apple's a rose,
And the pear is, and so's
The plum, I suppose.
The dear only knows
What will next prove a rose.
You, of course, are a rose –
But were always a rose.

ATMOSPHERE

Inscription for a garden wall

Winds blow the open grassy places bleak;
But where this old wall burns a sunny cheek,
They eddy over it too toppling weak
To blow the earth or anything self-clear;
Moisture and color and odor thicken here.
The hours of daylight gather atmosphere.

ON GOING UNNOTICED

As vain to raise a voice as a sigh
In the tumult of free leaves on high.
What are you, in the shadow of trees
Engaged up there with the light and breeze?

Less than the coralroot, you know,
That is content with the daylight low,
And has no leaves at all of its own;
Whose spotted flowers hang meanly down.

You grasp the bark by a rugged pleat,
And look up small from the forest's feet.
The only leaf it drops goes wide,
Your name not written on either side.

You linger your little hour and are gone,
And still the woods sweep leafily on,
Not even missing the coralroot flower
You took as a trophy of the hour.

THE COCOON

As far as I can see, this autumn haze
That spreading in the evening air both ways
Makes the new moon look anything but new
And pours the elm-tree meadow full of blue,
Is all the smoke from one poor house alone,
With but one chimney it can call its own;
So close it will not light an early light,
Keeping its life so close and out of sight
No one for hours has set a foot outdoors
So much as to take care of evening chores.
The inmates may be lonely womenfolk.
I want to tell them that with all this smoke
They prudently are spinning their cocoon
And anchoring it to an earth and moon
From which no winter gale can hope to blow it –
Spinning their own cocoon did they but know it.

A PASSING GLIMPSE

To Ridgely Torrence
on last looking into his 'Hesperides'

I often see flowers from a passing car
That are gone before I can tell what they are.

I want to get out of the train and go back
To see what they were beside the track.

I name all the flowers I am sure they weren't:
Not fireweed loving where woods have burnt –

Not bluebells gracing a tunnel mouth –
Not lupine living on sand and drouth.

Was something brushed across my mind
That no one on earth will ever find?

Heaven gives its glimpses only to those
Not in position to look too close.

A MINOR BIRD

I have wished a bird would fly away,
And not sing by my house all day;

Have clapped my hands at him from the door
When it seemed as if I could bear no more.

The fault must partly have been in me.
The bird was not to blame for his key.

And of course there must be something wrong
In wanting to silence any song.

BEREFT

Where had I heard this wind before
Change like this to a deeper roar?
What would it take my standing there for,
Holding open a restive door,
Looking downhill to a frothy shore?
Summer was past and day was past.
Somber clouds in the west were massed.
Out in the porch's sagging floor
Leaves got up in a coil and hissed,
Blindly struck at my knee and missed.
Something sinister in the tone

Told me my secret must be known:
Word I was in the house alone
Somehow must have gotten abroad,
Word I was in my life alone,
Word I had no one left but God.

TREE AT MY WINDOW

Tree at my window, window tree,
My sash is lowered when night comes on;
But let there never be curtain drawn
Between you and me.

Vague dream-head lifted out of the ground,
And thing next most diffuse to cloud,
Not all your light tongues talking aloud
Could be profound.

But, tree, I have seen you taken and tossed,
And if you have seen me when I slept,
You have seen me when I was taken and swept
And all but lost.

That day she put our heads together,
Fate had her imagination about her,
Your head so much concerned with outer,
Mine with inner, weather.

THE THATCH

Out alone in the winter rain,
Intent on giving and taking pain.
But never was I far out of sight

Of a certain upper-window light.
The light was what it was all about:
I would not go in till the light went out;
It would not go out till I came in.
Well, we should see which one would win,
We should see which one would be first to yield.
The world was a black invisible field.
The rain by rights was snow for cold.
The wind was another layer of mold.
But the strangest thing: in the thick old thatch,
Where summer birds had been given hatch,
Had fed in chorus, and lived to fledge,
Some still were living in hermitage.
And as I passed along the eaves
So low I brushed the straw with my sleeves,
I flushed birds out of hole after hole,
Into the darkness. It grieved my soul,
It started a grief within a grief,
To think their case was beyond relief –
They could not go flying about in search
Of their nest again, nor find a perch.
They must brood where they fell in mulch and mire,
Trusting feathers and inward fire
Till daylight made it safe for a flyer.
My greater grief was by so much reduced
As I thought of them without nest or roost.
That was how that grief started to melt.
They tell me the cottage where we dwelt,
Its wind-torn thatch goes now unmended;
Its life of hundreds of years has ended
By letting the rain I knew outdoors
In onto the upper chamber floors.

A WINTER EDEN

A winter garden in an alder swamp,
Where conies now come out to sun and romp,
As near a paradise as it can be
And not melt snow or start a dormant tree.

It lifts existence on a plane of snow
One level higher than the earth below,
One level nearer heaven overhead,
And last year's berries shining scarlet red.

It lifts a gaunt luxuriating beast
Where he can stretch and hold his highest feast
On some wild apple-tree's young tender bark,
What well may prove the year's high girdle mark.

So near to paradise all pairing ends:
Here loveless birds now flock as winter friends,
Content with bud-inspecting. They presume
To say which buds are leaf and which are bloom.

A feather-hammer gives a double knock.
This Eden day is done at two o'clock.
An hour of winter day might seem too short
To make it worth life's while to wake and sport.

THE FLOOD

Blood has been harder to dam back than water.
Just when we think we have it impounded safe
Behind new barrier walls (and let it chafe!),
It breaks away in some new kind of slaughter.
We choose to say it is let loose by the devil;

But power of blood itself releases blood.
It goes by might of being such a flood
Held high at so unnatural a level.
It will have outlet, brave and not so brave.
Weapons of war and implements of peace
Are but the points at which it finds release.
And now it is once more the tidal wave
That when it has swept by, leaves summits stained.
Oh, blood will out. It cannot be contained.

ACQUAINTED WITH THE NIGHT

I have been one acquainted with the night.
I have walked out in rain – and back in rain.
I have outwalked the furthest city light.

I have looked down the saddest city lane.
I have passed by the watchman on his beat
And dropped my eyes, unwilling to explain.

I have stood still and stopped the sound of feet
When far away an interrupted cry
Came over houses from another street,

But not to call me back or say good-by;
And further still at an unearthly height
One luminary clock against the sky

Proclaimed the time was neither wrong nor right.
I have been one acquainted with the night.

'Fred, where is north?'

'North? North is there, my love.
The brook runs west.'

'West-Running Brook then call it.'
(West-Running Brook men call it to this day.)
'What does it think it's doing running west
When all the other country brooks flow east
To reach the ocean? It must be the brook
Can trust itself to go by contraries
The way I can with you – and you with me –
Because we're – we're – I don't know what we are.
What are we?'

'Young or new?'

'We must be something.
We've said we two. Let's change that to we three.
As you and I are married to each other,
We'll both be married to the brook. We'll build
Our bridge across it, and the bridge shall be
Our arm thrown over it asleep beside it.
Look, look, it's waving to us with a wave
To let us know it hears me.'

'Why, my dear,
That wave's been standing off this jut of shore –'
(The black stream, catching on a sunken rock,
Flung backward on itself in one white wave,
And the white water rode the black forever,
Not gaining but not losing, like a bird
White feathers from the struggle of whose breast
Flecked the dark stream and flecked the darker pool
Below the point, and were at last driven wrinkled

In a white scarf against the far-shore alders.)
'That wave's been standing off this jut of shore
Ever since rivers, I was going to say,
Were made in heaven. It wasn't waved to us.'

'It wasn't, yet it was. If not to you,
It was to me – in an annunciation.'

'Oh, if you take it off to lady-land,
As't were the country of the Amazons
We men must see you to the confines of
And leave you there, ourselves forbid to enter –
It is your brook! I have no more to say.'

'Yes, you have, too. Go on. You thought of something.'

'Speaking of contraries, see how the brook
In that white wave runs counter to itself.
It is from that in water we were from
Long, long before we were from any creature.
Here we, in our impatience of the steps,
Get back to the beginning of beginnings,
The stream of everything that runs away.
Some say existence like a Pirouot
And Pirouette, forever in one place,
Stands still and dances, but it runs away;
It seriously, sadly, runs away
To fill the abyss's void with emptiness.
It flows beside us in this water brook,
But it flows over us. It flows between us
To separate us for a panic moment.
It flows between us, over us, and *with* us.
And it is time, strength, tone, light, life, and love –
And even substance lapsing unsubstantial;
The universal cataract of death
That spends to nothingness – and unresisted,
Save by some strange resistance in itself,

Not just a swerving, but a throwing back,
As if regret were in it and were sacred.
It has this throwing backward on itself
So that the fall of most of it is always
Raising a little, sending up a little.
Our life runs down in sending up the clock.
The brook runs down in sending up our life.
The sun runs down in sending up the brook.
And there is something sending up the sun.
It is this backward motion toward the source,
Against the stream, that most we see ourselves in,
The tribute of the current to the source.
It is from this in nature we are from.
It is most us.'

'Today will be the day
You said so.'

'No, today will be the day
You said the brook was called West-Running Brook.'

'Today will be the day of what we both said.'

A SOLDIER

He is that fallen lance that lies as hurled,
That lies unlifted now, come dew, come rust,
But still lies pointed as it plowed the dust.
If we who sight along it round the world,
See nothing worthy to have been its mark,
It is because like men we look too near,
Forgetting that as fitted to the sphere,
Our missiles always make too short an arc.
They fall, they rip the grass, they intersect
The curve of earth, and striking, break their own;

They make us cringe for metal-point on stone.
But this we know, the obstacle that checked
And tripped the body, shot the spirit on
Further than target ever showed or shone.

IMMIGRANTS

No ship of all that under sail or steam
Have gathered people to us more and more
But, Pilgrim-manned, the *Mayflower* in a dream
Has been her anxious convoy in to shore.

HANNIBAL

Was there ever a cause too lost,
Ever a cause that was lost too long,
Or that showed with the lapse of time too vain
For the generous tears of youth and song?

THE LAST MOWING

There's a place called Faraway Meadow
We never shall mow in again,
Or such is the talk at the farmhouse:
The meadow is finished with men.
Then now is the chance for the flowers
That can't stand mowers and plowers.
It must be now, though, in season
Before the not mowing brings trees on,
Before trees, seeing the opening,
March into a shadowy claim.
The trees are all I'm afraid of,

That flowers can't bloom in the shade of;
It's no more men I'm afraid of;
The meadow is done with the tame.
The place for the moment is ours
For you, O tumultuous flowers,
To go to waste and go wild in,
All shapes and colors of flowers,
I needn't call you by name.

THE BIRTHPLACE

Here further up the mountain slope
Than there was ever any hope,
My father built, enclosed a spring,
Strung chains of wall round everything,
Subdued the growth of earth to grass,
And brought our various lives to pass.
A dozen girls and boys we were.
The mountain seemed to like the stir,
And made of us a little while –
With always something in her smile.
Today she wouldn't know our name.
(No girl's, of course, has stayed the same.)
The mountain pushed us off her knees.
And now her lap is full of trees.

THE DOOR IN THE DARK

In going from room to room in the dark
I reached out blindly to save my face,
But neglected, however lightly, to lace
My fingers and close my arms in an arc.
A slim door got in past my guard,

And hit me a blow in the head so hard
I had my native simile jarred.
So people and things don't pair anymore
With what they used to pair with before.

THE BEAR

The bear puts both arms around the tree above her
And draws it down as if it were a lover
And its chokecherries lips to kiss good-by,
Then lets it snap back upright in the sky.
Her next step rocks a boulder on the wall
(She's making her cross-country in the fall).
Her great weight creaks the barbed wire in its staples
As she flings over and off down through the maples,
Leaving on one wire tooth a lock of hair.
Such is the uncaged progress of the bear.
The world has room to make a bear feel free;
The universe seems cramped to you and me.
Man acts more like the poor bear in a cage,
That all day fights a nervous inward rage,
His mood rejecting all his mind suggests.
He paces back and forth and never rests
The toenail click and shuffle of his feet,
The telescope at one end of his beat,
And at the other end the microscope,
Two instruments of nearly equal hope,
And in conjunction giving quite a spread.
Or if he rests from scientific tread,
'Tis only to sit back and sway his head
Through ninety-odd degrees of arc, it seems,
Between two metaphysical extremes.
He sits back on his fundamental butt
With lifted snout and eyes (if any) shut

(He almost looks religious but he's not),
And back and forth he sways from cheek to cheek,
At one extreme agreeing with one Greek,
At the other agreeing with another Greek,
Which may be thought, but only so to speak.
A baggy figure, equally pathetic
When sedentary and when peripatetic.

A FURTHER RANGE

1936

A LONE STRIKER

The swinging mill bell changed its rate
To tolling like the count of fate,
And though at that the tardy ran,
One failed to make the closing gate.
There was a law of God or man
That on the one who came too late
The gate for half an hour be locked,
His time be lost, his pittance docked.
He stood rebuked and unemployed.
The straining mill began to shake.
The mill, though many-many-eyed,
Had eyes inscrutably opaque;
So that he couldn't look inside
To see if some forlorn machine
Was standing idle for his sake.
(He couldn't hope its heart would break.)

And yet he thought he saw the scene:
The air was full of dust of wool.
A thousand yarns were under pull,
But pull so slow, with such a twist,
All day from spool to lesser spool,
It seldom overtaxed their strength;
They safely grew in slender length.
And if one broke by any chance,
The spinner saw it at a glance.
The spinner still was there to spin.
That's where the human still came in.
Her deft hand showed with finger rings
Among the harplike spread of strings.
She caught the pieces end to end

And, with a touch that never missed,
Not so much tied as made them blend.
Man's ingenuity was good.
He saw it plainly where he stood,
Yet found it easy to resist.

He knew another place, a wood,
And in it, tall as trees, were cliffs;
And if he stood on one of these,
'Twould be among the tops of trees,
Their upper branches round him wreathing,
Their breathing mingled with his breathing.
If – if he stood! Enough of ifs!
He knew a path that wanted walking;
He knew a spring that wanted drinking;
A thought that wanted further thinking;
A love that wanted re-renewing.
Nor was this just a way of talking
To save him the expense of doing.
With him it boded action, deed.

The factory was very fine;
He wished it all the modern speed.
Yet, after all, 'twas not divine,
That is to say, 'twas not a church.
He never would assume that he'd
Be any institution's need.
But he said then and still would say,
If there should ever come a day
When industry seemed like to die
Because he left it in the lurch,
Or even merely seemed to pine
For want of his approval, why,
Come get him – they knew where to search.

TWO TRAMPS IN MUD TIME

Out of the mud two strangers came
And caught me splitting wood in the yard.
And one of them put me off my aim
By hailing cheerily 'Hit them hard!'
I knew pretty well why he dropped behind
And let the other go on a way.
I knew pretty well what he had in mind:
He wanted to take my job for pay.

Good blocks of oak it was I split,
As large around as the chopping block;
And every piece I squarely hit
Fell splinterless as a cloven rock.
The blows that a life of self-control
Spares to strike for the common good,
That day, giving a loose to my soul,
I spent on the unimportant wood.

The sun was warm but the wind was chill.
You know how it is with an April day
When the sun is out and the wind is still,
You're one month on in the middle of May.
But if you so much as dare to speak,
A cloud comes over the sunlit arch,
A wind comes off a frozen peak,
And you're two months back in the middle of March.

A bluebird comes tenderly up to alight
And turns to the wind to unruffle a plume,
His song so pitched as not to excite
A single flower as yet to bloom.
It is snowing a flake: and he half knew
Winter was only playing possum.

Except in color he isn't blue,
But he wouldn't advise a thing to blossom.

The water for which we may have to look
In summertime with a witching wand,
In every wheelrut's now a brook,
In every print of a hoof a pond.
Be glad of water, but don't forget
The lurking frost in the earth beneath
That will steal forth after the sun is set
And show on the water its crystal teeth.

The time when most I loved my task
These two must make me love it more
By coming with what they came to ask.
You'd think I never had felt before
The weight of an ax-head poised aloft,
The grip on earth of outspread feet,
The life of muscles rocking soft
And smooth and moist in vernal heat.

Out of the woods two hulking tramps
(From sleeping God knows where last night,
But not long since in the lumber camps).
They thought all chopping was theirs of right.
Men of the woods and lumberjacks,
They judged me by their appropriate tool.
Except as a fellow handled an ax
They had no way of knowing a fool.

Nothing on either side was said.
They knew they had but to stay their stay
And all their logic would fill my head:
As that I had no right to play
With what was another man's work for gain.

My right might be love but theirs was need.
And where the two exist in twain
Theirs was the better right – agreed.

But yield who will to their separation,
My object in living is to unite
My avocation and my vocation
As my two eyes make one in sight.
Only where love and need are one,
And the work is play for mortal stakes,
Is the deed ever really done
For Heaven and the future's sakes.

THE WHITE-TAILED HORNET

The white-tailed hornet lives in a balloon
That floats against the ceiling of the woodshed.
The exit he comes out at like a bullet
Is like the pupil of a pointed gun.
And having power to change his aim in flight,
He comes out more unerring than a bullet.
Verse could be written on the certainty
With which he penetrates my best defense
Of whirling hands and arms about the head
To stab me in the sneeze-nerve of a nostril.
Such is the instinct of it I allow.
Yet how about the insect certainty
That in the neighborhood of home and children
Is such an execrable judge of motives
As not to recognize in me the exception
I like to think I am in everything –
One who would never hang above a bookcase
His Japanese crepe-paper globe for trophy?
He stung me first and stung me afterward.

He rolled me off the field head over heels
And would not listen to my explanations.

That's when I went as visitor to his house.
As visitor at my house he is better.
Hawking for flies about the kitchen door,
In at one door perhaps and out another,
Trust him then not to put you in the wrong.
He won't misunderstand your freest movements.
Let him light on your skin unless you mind
So many prickly grappling feet at once.
He's after the domesticated fly
To feed his thumping grubs as big as he is.
Here he is at his best, but even here –
I watched him where he swooped, he pounced, he struck;
But what he found he had was just a nailhead.
He struck a second time. Another nailhead.
'Those are just nailheads. Those are fastened down.'
Then disconcerted and not unannoyed,
He stooped and struck a little huckleberry
The way a player curls around a football.
'Wrong shape, wrong color, and wrong scent,' I said.
The huckleberry rolled him on his head.
At last it was a fly. He shot and missed;
And the fly circled round him in derision.
But for the fly he might have made me think
He had been at his poetry, comparing
Nailhead with fly and fly with huckleberry:
How like a fly, how very like a fly.
But the real fly he missed would never do;
The missed fly made me dangerously skeptic.

Won't this whole instinct matter bear revision?
Won't almost any theory bear revision?
To err is human, not to, animal.

Or so we pay the compliment to instinct,
Only too liberal of our compliment
That really takes away instead of gives.
Our worship, humor, conscientiousness
Went long since to the dogs under the table.
And served us right for having instituted
Downward comparisons. As long on earth
As our comparisons were stoutly upward
With gods and angels, we were men at least,
But little lower than the gods and angels.
But once comparisons were yielded downward,
Once we began to see our images
Reflected in the mud and even dust,
'Twas disillusion upon disillusion.
We were lost piecemeal to the animals,
Like people thrown out to delay the wolves.
Nothing but fallibility was left us,
And this day's work made even that seem doubtful.

A DRUMLIN WOODCHUCK

One thing has a shelving bank,
Another a rotting plank,
To give it cozier skies
And make up for its lack of size.

My own strategic retreat
Is where two rocks almost meet,
And still more secure and snug,
A two-door burrow I dug.

With those in mind at my back
I can sit forth exposed to attack,
As one who shrewdly pretends
That he and the world are friends.

All we who prefer to live
Have a little whistle we give,
And flash, at the least alarm
We dive down under the farm.

We allow some time for guile
And don't come out for a while,
Either to eat or drink.
We take occasion to think.

And if after the hunt goes past
And the double-barreled blast
(Like war and pestilence
And the loss of common sense),

If I can with confidence say
That still for another day,
Or even another year,
I will be there for you, my dear,

It will be because, though small
As measured against the All,
I have been so instinctively thorough
About my crevice and burrow.

DEPARTMENTAL

An ant on the tablecloth
Ran into a dormant moth
Of many times his size.
He showed not the least surprise.
His business wasn't with such.
He gave it scarcely a touch,
And was off on his duty run.
Yet if he encountered one

Of the hive's enquiry squad
Whose work is to find out God
And the nature of time and space,
He would put him onto the case.
Ants are a curious race;
One crossing with hurried tread
The body of one of their dead
Isn't given a moment's arrest –
Seems not even impressed.
But he no doubt reports to any
With whom he crosses antennae,
And they no doubt report
To the higher-up at court.
Then word goes forth in Formic:
'Death's come to Jerry McCormic,
Our selfless forager Jerry.
Will the special Janizary
Whose office it is to bury
The dead of the commissary
Go bring him home to his people.
Lay him in state on a sepal.
Wrap him for shroud in a petal.
Embalm him with ichor of nettle.
This is the word of your Queen.'
And presently on the scene
Appears a solemn mortician;
And taking formal position,
With feelers calmly atwiddle,
Seizes the dead by the middle,
And heaving him high in air,
Carries him out of there.
No one stands round to stare.
It is nobody else's affair.

It couldn't be called ungentle.
But how thoroughly departmental.

ON THE HEART'S BEGINNING TO CLOUD THE MIND

Something I saw or thought I saw
In the desert at midnight in Utah,
Looking out of my lower berth
At moonlit sky and moonlit earth.
The sky had here and there a star;
The earth had a single light afar,
A flickering, human pathetic light,
That was maintained against the night,
It seemed to me, by the people there,
With a Godforsaken brute despair.
It would flutter and fall in half an hour
Like the last petal off a flower.
But my heart was beginning to cloud my mind.
I knew a tale of a better kind.
That far light flickers because of trees.
The people can burn it as long as they please;
And when their interests in it end,
They can leave it to someone else to tend.
Come back that way a summer hence,
I should find it no more no less intense.
I pass, but scarcely pass no doubt,
When one will say, 'Let us put it out.'
The other without demur agrees.
They can keep it burning as long as they please;
They can put it out whenever they please.
One looks out last from the darkened room
At the shiny desert with spots of gloom
That might be people and are but cedar,
Have no purpose, have no leader,
Have never made the first move to assemble,
And so are nothing to make her tremble.
She can think of places that are not thus

Without indulging a 'Not for us!'
Life is not so sinister-grave.
Matter of fact has made them brave.
He is husband, she is wife.
She fears not him, they fear not life.
They know where another light has been,
And more than one, to theirs akin,
But earlier out for bed tonight,
So lost on me in my surface flight.

This I saw when waking late,
Going by at a railroad rate,
Looking through wreaths of engine smoke
Far into the lives of other folk.

AT WOODWARD'S GARDENS

A boy, presuming on his intellect,
Once showed two little monkeys in a cage
A burning-glass they could not understand
And never could be made to understand.
Words are no good: to say it was a lens
For gathering solar rays would not have helped.
But let him show them how the weapon worked.
He made the sun a pinpoint on the nose
Of first one, then the other, till it brought
A look of puzzled dimness to their eyes
That blinking could not seem to blink away.
They stood arms laced together at the bars,
And exchanged troubled glances over life.
One put a thoughtful hand up to his nose
As if reminded – or as if perhaps
Within a million years of an idea.
He got his purple little knuckles stung.
The already known had once more been confirmed

By psychological experiment,
And that were all the finding to announce
Had the boy not presumed too close and long.
There was a sudden flash of arm, a snatch,
And the glass was the monkeys', not the boy's.
Precipitately they retired back-cage
And instituted an investigation
On their part, though without the needed insight.
They bit the glass and listened for the flavor.
They broke the handle and the binding off it.
Then none the wiser, frankly gave it up,
And having hid it in their bedding straw
Against the day of prisoners' ennui,
Came dryly forward to the bars again
To answer for themselves: Who said it mattered
What monkeys did or didn't understand?
They might not understand a burning-glass.
They might not understand the sun itself.
It's knowing what to do with things that counts.

LOST IN HEAVEN

The clouds, the source of rain, one stormy night
Offered an opening to the source of dew;
Which I accepted with impatient sight,
Looking for my old sky-marks in the blue.

But stars were scarce in that part of the sky,
And no two were of the same constellation –
No one was bright enough to identify;
So 'twas with not ungrateful consternation,

Seeing myself well lost once more, I sighed,
'Where, where in Heaven am I? But don't tell me!

O opening clouds, by opening on me wide.
Let's let my heavenly lostness overwhelm me.'

DESERT PLACES

Snow falling and night falling fast, oh, fast
In a field I looked into going past,
And the ground almost covered smooth in snow,
But a few weeds and stubble showing last.

The woods around it have it – it is theirs.
All animals are smothered in their lairs.
I am too absent-spirited to count;
The loneliness includes me unawares.

And lonely as it is, that loneliness
Will be more lonely ere it will be less –
A blanker whiteness of benighted snow
With no expression, nothing to express.

They cannot scare me with their empty spaces
Between stars – on stars where no human race is.
I have it in me so much nearer home
To scare myself with my own desert places.

A LEAF-TREADER

I have been treading on leaves all day until I am autumn-tired.
God knows all the color and form of leaves I have trodden on
  and mired.
Perhaps I have put forth too much strength and been too fierce
  from fear.
I have safely trodden underfoot the leaves of another year.

All summer long they were overhead, more lifted up than I.
To come to their final place in earth they had to pass me by.
All summer long I thought I heard them threatening under their breath.
And when they came it seemed with a will to carry me with them to death.

They spoke to the fugitive in my heart as if it were leaf to leaf.
They tapped at my eyelids and touched my lips with an invitation to grief.
But it was no reason I had to go because they had to go.
Now up, my knee, to keep on top of another year of snow.

THEY WERE WELCOME TO THEIR BELIEF

Grief may have thought it was grief.
Care may have thought it was care.
They were welcome to their belief,
The overimportant pair.

No, it took all the snows that clung
To the low roof over his bed,
Beginning when he was young,
To induce the one snow on his head.

But whenever the roof came white
The head in the dark below
Was a shade less the color of night,
A shade more the color of snow.

Grief may have thought it was grief.
Care may have thought it was care.
But neither one was the thief
Of his raven color of hair.

THE STRONG ARE SAYING NOTHING

The soil now gets a rumpling soft and damp,
And small regard to the future of any weed.
The final flat of the hoe's approval stamp
Is reserved for the bed of a few selected seed.

There is seldom more than a man to a harrowed piece.
Men work alone, their lots plowed far apart,
One stringing a chair of seed in an open crease,
And another stumbling after a halting cart.

To the fresh and black of the squares of early mold
The leafless bloom of a plum is fresh and white;
Though there's more than a doubt if the weather is not too cold
For the bees to come and serve its beauty aright.

Wind goes from farm to farm in wave on wave,
But carries no cry of what is hoped to be.
There may be little or much beyond the grave,
But the strong are saying nothing until they see.

THE MASTER SPEED

No speed of wind or water rushing by
But you have speed far greater. You can climb
Back up a stream of radiance to the sky,
And back through history up the stream of time.
And you were given this swiftness, not for haste
Nor chiefly that you may go where you will,
But in the rush of everything to waste,
That you may have the power of standing still –
Off any still or moving thing you say.
Two such as you with such a master speed

Cannot be parted nor be swept away
From one another once you are agreed
That life is only life forevermore
Together wing to wing and oar to oar.

MOON COMPASSES

I stole forth dimly in the dripping pause
Between two downpours to see what there was.
And a masked moon had spread down compass rays
To a cone mountain in the midnight haze,
As if the final estimate were hers;
And as it measured in her calipers,
The mountain stood exalted in its place.
So love will take between the hands a face . . .

NEITHER OUT FAR NOR IN DEEP

The people along the sand
All turn and look one way.
They turn their back on the land.
They look at the sea all day.

As long as it takes to pass
A ship keeps raising its hull;
The wetter ground like glass
Reflects a standing gull.

The land may vary more;
But wherever the truth may be –
The water comes ashore,
And the people look at the sea.

They cannot look out far.
They cannot look in deep.
But when was that ever a bar
To any watch they keep?

DESIGN

I found a dimpled spider, fat and white,
On a white heal-all, holding up a moth
Like a white piece of rigid satin cloth –
Assorted characters of death and blight
Mixed ready to begin the morning right,
Like the ingredients of a witches' broth –
A snow-drop spider, a flower like a froth,
And dead wings carried like a paper kite.

What had that flower to do with being white,
The wayside blue and innocent heal-all?
What brought the kindred spider to that height,
Then steered the white moth thither in the night?
What but design of darkness to appall? –
If design govern in a thing so small.

ON A BIRD SINGING IN ITS SLEEP

A bird half wakened in the lunar noon
Sang halfway through its little inborn tune.
Partly because it sang but once all night
And that from no especial bush's height,
Partly because it sang ventriloquist
And had the inspiration to desist
Almost before the prick of hostile ears,
It ventured less in peril than appears.

It could not have come down to us so far,
Through the interstices of things ajar
On the long bead chain of repeated birth,
To be a bird while we are men on earth,
If singing out of sleep and dream that way
Had made it much more easily a prey.

AFTERFLAKES

In the thick of a teeming snowfall
I saw my shadow on snow.
I turned and looked back up at the sky,
Where we still look to ask the why
Of everything below.

If I shed such a darkness,
If the reason was in me,
That shadow of mine should show in form
Against the shapeless shadow of storm,
How swarthy I must be.

I turned and looked back upward.
The whole sky was blue;
And the thick flakes floating at a pause
Were but frost knots on an airy gauze,
With the sun shining through.

UNHARVESTED

A scent of ripeness from over a wall.
And come to leave the routine road
And look for what had made me stall,
There sure enough was an apple tree

That had eased itself of its summer load,
And of all but its trivial foliage free,
Now breathed as light as a lady's fan.
For there there had been an apple fall
As complete as the apple had given man.
The ground was one circle of solid red.

May something go always unharvested!
May much stay out of our stated plan,
Apples or something forgotten and left,
So smelling their sweetness would be no theft.

THERE ARE ROUGHLY ZONES

We sit indoors and talk of the cold outside.
And every gust that gathers strength and heaves
Is a threat to the house. But the house has long been tried.
We think of the tree. If it never again has leaves,
We'll know, we say, that this was the night it died.
It is very far north, we admit, to have brought the peach.
What comes over a man, is it soul or mind –
That to no limits and bounds he can stay confined?
You would say his ambition was to extend the reach
Clear to the Arctic of every living kind.
Why is his nature forever so hard to teach
That though there is no fixed line between wrong and right,
There are roughly zones whose laws must be obeyed?
There is nothing much we can do for the tree tonight,
But we can't help feeling more than a little betrayed
That the northwest wind should rise to such a height
Just when the cold went down so many below.
The tree has no leaves and may never have them again.
We must wait till some months hence in the spring to know.
But if it is destined never again to grow,
It can blame this limitless trait in the hearts of men.

NOT QUITE SOCIAL

Some of you will be glad I did what I did,
And the rest won't want to punish me too severely
For finding a thing to do that though not forbid
Yet wasn't enjoined and wasn't expected, clearly.

To punish me overcruelly wouldn't be right
For merely giving you once more gentle proof
That the city's hold on a man is no more tight
Than when its walls rose higher than any roof.

You may taunt me with not being able to flee the earth.
You have me there, but loosely, as I would be held.
The way of understanding is partly mirth.
I would not be taken as ever having rebelled.

And anyone is free to condemn me to death –
If he leaves it to nature to carry out the sentence.
I shall will to the common stock of air my breath
And pay a death tax of fairly polite repentance.

BUILD SOIL

A political pastoral

Why, Tityrus! But you've forgotten me.
I'm Meliboeus the potato man,
The one you had the talk with, you remember,
Here on this very campus years ago.
Hard times have struck me and I'm on the move.
I've had to give my interval farm up
For interest, and I've bought a mountain farm
For nothing down, all-out-doors of a place,
All woods and pasture only fit for sheep.

But sheep is what I'm going into next.
I'm done forever with potato crops
At thirty cents a bushel. Give me sheep.
I know wool's down to seven cents a pound.
But I don't calculate to sell my wool.
I didn't my potatoes. I consumed them.
I'll dress up in sheep's clothing and eat sheep.
The Muse takes care of you. You live by writing
Your poems on a farm and call that farming.
Oh, I don't blame you. I say take life easy.
I should myself, only I don't know how.
But have some pity on us who have to work.
Why don't you use your talents as a writer
To advertise our farms to city buyers,
Or else write something to improve food prices.
Get in a poem toward the next election.

Oh, Meliboeus, I have half a mind
To take a writing hand in politics.
Before now poetry has taken notice
Of wars, and what are wars but politics
Transformed from chronic to acute and bloody?

I may be wrong, but, Tityrus, to me
The times seem revolutionary bad.

The question is whether they've reached a depth
Of desperation that would warrant poetry's
Leaving love's alternations, joy and grief,
The weather's alternations, summer and winter,
Our age-long theme, for the uncertainty
Of judging who is a contemporary liar –
Who in particular, when all alike
Get called as much in clashes of ambition.
Life may be tragically bad, and I
Make bold to sing it so, but do I dare

Name names and tell you who by name is wicked?
Whittier's luck with Skipper Ireson awes me –
Many men's luck with Greatest Washington
(Who sat for Stuart's portrait, but who sat
Equally for the nation's Constitution).
I prefer to sing safely in the realm
Of types, composite and imagined people:
To affirm there is such a thing as evil
Personified, but ask to be excused
From saying on a jury 'Here's the guilty.'

I doubt if you're convinced the times are bad.

I keep my eye on Congress, Meliboeus.
They're in the best position of us all
To know if anything is very wrong.
I mean they could be trusted to give the alarm
If earth were thought about to change its axis,
Or a star coming to dilate the sun.
As long as lightly all their livelong sessions,
Like a yardful of schoolboys out at recess
Before their plays and games were organized,
They yelling mix tag, hide-and-seek, hopscotch,
And leapfrog in each other's way – all's well.
Let newspapers profess to fear the worst!
Nothing's portentous, I am reassured.

Is socialism needed, do you think?

We have it now. For socialism is
An element in any government.
There's no such thing as socialism pure –
Except as an abstraction of the mind.
There's only democratic socialism,
Monarchic socialism, oligarchic –

The last being what they seem to have in Russia.
You often get it most in monarchy,
Least in democracy. In practice, pure,
I don't know what it would be. No one knows.
I have no doubt like all the loves when
Philosophized together into one –
One sickness of the body and the soul.
Thank God our practice holds the loves apart,
Beyond embarrassing self-consciousness
Where natural friends are met, where dogs are kept,
Where women pray with priests. There is no love.
There's only love of men and women, love
Of children, love of friends, of men, of God:
Divine love, human love, parental love,
Roughly discriminated for the rough.

Poetry, itself once more, is back in love.

Pardon the analogy, my Meliboeus,
For sweeping me away. Let's see, where was I?

But don't you think more should be socialized
Than is?

What should you mean by socialized?

Made good for everyone – things like inventions –
Made so we all should get the good of them –
All, not just great exploiting businesses.

We sometimes only get the bad of them.
In your sense of the word ambition has
Been socialized – the first propensity
To be attempted. Greed may well come next.
But the worst one of all to leave uncurbed,

Unsocialized, is ingenuity:
Which for no sordid self-aggrandizement,
For nothing but its own blind satisfaction
(In this it is as much like hate as love),
Works in the dark as much against as for us.
Even while we talk some chemist at Columbia
Is stealthily contriving wool from jute
That when let loose upon the grazing world
Will put ten thousand farmers out of sheep.
Everyone asks for freedom for himself,
The man free love, the businessman free trade,
The writer and talker free speech and free press.
Political ambition has been taught,
By being punished back, it is not free:
It must at some point gracefully refrain.
Greed has been taught a little abnegation
And shall be more before we're done with it.
It is just fool enough to think itself
Self-taught. But our brute snarling and lashing taught it.
None shall be as ambitious as he can.
None should be as ingenious as he could,
Not if I had my say. Bounds should be set
To ingenuity for being so cruel
In bringing change unheralded on the unready.

I elect you to put the curb on it.

Were I dictator, I'll tell you what I'd do.

What should you do?

                                        I'd let things take their course
And then I'd claim the credit for the outcome.

You'd make a sort of safety-first dictator.

Don't let the things I say against myself
Betray you into taking sides against me,
Or it might get you into trouble with me.
I'm not afraid to prophesy the future,
And be judged by the outcome, Meliboeus.
Listen and I will take my dearest risk.
We're always too much out or too much in.
At present from a cosmical dilation
We're so much out that the odds are against
Our ever getting inside in again.
But inside in is where we've got to get.
My friends all know I'm interpersonal.
But long before I'm interpersonal,
Away 'way down inside I'm personal.
Just so before we're international,
We're national and act as nationals.
The colors are kept unmixed on the palette,
Or better on dish plates all around the room,
So the effect when they are mixed on canvas
May seem almost exclusively designed.
Some minds are so confounded intermental
They remind me of pictures on a palette:
'Look at what happened. Surely some god *pinxit*.
Come look at my significant mud pie.'
It's hard to tell which is the worse abhorrence,
Whether it's persons pied or nations pied.
Don't let me seem to say the exchange, the encounter,
May not be the important thing at last.
It well may be. We meet – I don't say when –
But must bring to the meeting the maturest,
The longest-saved-up, raciest, localest
We have strength of reserve in us to bring.

Tityrus, sometimes I'm perplexed myself
To find the good of commerce. Why should I

Have to sell you my apples and buy yours?
It can't be just to give the robber a chance
To catch them and take toll of them in transit.
Too mean a thought to get much comfort out of.
I figure that like any bandying
Of words or toys, it ministers to health.
It very likely quickens and refines us.

To market 'tis our destiny to go.
But much as in the end we bring for sale there,
There is still more we never bring or should bring;
More that should be kept back – the soil for instance,
In my opinion – though we both know poets
Who fall all over each other to bring soil
And even subsoil and hardpan to market.
To sell the hay off, let alone the soil,
Is an unpardonable sin in farming.
The moral is, make a late start to market.
Let me preach to you, will you, Meliboeus?

Preach on. I thought you were already preaching.
But preach and see if I can tell the difference.

Needless to say to you, my argument
Is not to lure the city to the country.
Let those possess the land, and only those,
Who love it with a love so strong and stupid
That they may be abused and taken advantage of
And made fun of by business, law, and art;
They still hang on. That so much of the earth's
Unoccupied need not make us uneasy.
We don't pretend to complete occupancy.
The world's one globe, human society
Another softer globe that slightly flattened
Rests on the world, and clinging slowly rolls.
We have our own round shape to keep unbroken.

The world's size has no more to do with us
Than has the universe's. We are balls,
We are round from the same source of roundness.
We are both round because the mind is round,
Because all reasoning is in a circle.
At least that's why the universe is round.

If what you're preaching is a line of conduct,
Just what am I supposed to do about it?
Reason in circles?

No, refuse to be
Seduced back to the land by any claim
The land may seem to have on man to use it.
Let none assume to till the land but farmers.
I only speak to you as one of them.
You shall go to your run-out mountain farm,
Poor castaway of commerce, and so live
That none shall ever see you come to market –
Not for a long, long time. Plant, breed, produce,
But what you raise or grow, why, feed it out,
Eat it or plow it under where it stands,
To build the soil. For what is more accursed
Than an impoverished soil, pale and metallic?
What cries more to our kind for sympathy?
I'll make a compact with you, Meliboeus,
To match you deed for deed and plan for plan.
Friends crowd around me with their five-year plans
That Soviet Russia has made fashionable.
You come to me and I'll unfold to you
A five-year plan I call so not because
It takes ten years or so to carry out,
Rather because it took five years at least
To think it out. Come close, let us conspire –
In self-restraint, if in restraint of trade.

You will go to your run-out mountain farm
And do what I command you. I take care
To command only what you meant to do
Anyway. That is my style of dictator.
Build soil. Turn the farm in upon itself
Until it can contain itself no more,
But sweating-full, drips wine and oil a little.
I will go to my run-out social mind
And be as unsocial with it as I can.
The thought I have, and my first impulse is
To take to market – I will turn it under.
The thought from that thought – I will turn it under.
And so on to the limit of my nature.
We are too much out, and if we won't draw in
We shall be driven in. I was brought up
A state-rights free-trade Democrat. What's that?
An inconsistency. The state shall be
Laws to itself, it seems, and yet have no
Control of what it sells or what it buys.
Suppose someone comes near me who in rate
Of speech and thinking is so much my better
I am imposed on, silenced and discouraged.
Do I submit to being supplied by him
As the more economical producer,
More wonderful, more beautiful producer?
No. I unostentatiously move off
Far enough for my thought-flow to resume.
Thought product and food product are to me
Nothing compared to the producing of them.
I sent you once a song with the refrain:

> Let me be the one
> To do what is done –

My share at least, lest I be empty-idle.
Keep off each other and keep each other off.

You see the beauty of my proposal is
It needn't wait on general revolution.
I bid you to a one-man revolution –
The only revolution that is coming.
We're too unseparate out among each other –
With goods to sell and notions to impart.
A youngster comes to me with half a quatrain
To ask me if I think it worth the pains
Of working out the rest, the other half.
I am brought guaranteed young prattle poems
Made publicly in school, above suspicion
Of plagiarism and help of cheating parents.
We congregate embracing from distrust
As much as love, and too close in to strike
And be so very striking. Steal away,
The song says. Steal away and stay away.
Don't join too many gangs. Join few if any.
Join the United States and join the family –
But not much in between unless a college.
Is it a bargain, Shepherd Meliboeus?

Probably, but you're far too fast and strong
For my mind to keep working in your presence.
I can tell better after I get home,
Better a month from now when cutting posts
Or mending fence it all comes back to me
What I was thinking when you interrupted
My life-train logic. I agree with you
We're too unseparate. And going home
From company means coming to our senses.

TO A THINKER

The last step taken found your heft
Decidedly upon the left.

One more would throw you on the right.
Another still – you see your plight.
You call this thinking, but it's walking.
Not even that, it's only rocking,
Or weaving like a stabled horse:
From force to matter and back to force,
From form to content and back to form,
From norm to crazy and back to norm,
From bound to free and back to bound,
From sound to sense and back to sound.
So back and forth. It almost scares
A man the way things come in pairs.
Just now you're off democracy
(With a polite regret to be)
And leaning on dictatorship;
But if you will accept the tip,
In less than no time, tongue and pen,
You'll be a democrat again.
A reasoner and good as such,
Don't let it bother you too much
If it makes you look helpless, please,
And a temptation to the tease.
Suppose you've no direction in you,
I don't see but you must continue
To use the gift you do possess,
And sway with reason more or less.
I own I never really warmed
To the reformer or reformed.
And yet conversion has its place
Not halfway down the scale of grace.
So if you find you must repent
From side to side in argument,
At least don't use your mind too hard,
But trust my instinct – I'm a bard.

A WITNESS TREE

1942

BEECH

Where my imaginary line
Bends square in woods, an iron spine
And pile of real rocks have been founded.
And off this corner in the wild,
Where these are driven in and piled,
One tree, by being deeply wounded,
Has been impressed as Witness Tree
And made commit to memory
My proof of being not unbounded.
Thus truth's established and borne out,
Though circumstanced with dark and doubt –
Though by a world of doubt surrounded.

– *The Moodie Forester*

COME IN

As I came to the edge of the woods,
Thrush music – hark!
Now if it was dusk outside,
Inside it was dark.

Too dark in the woods for a bird
By sleight of wing
To better its perch for the night,
Though it still could sing.

The last of the light of the sun
That had died in the west
Still lived for one song more
In a thrush's breast.

Far in the pillared dark
Thrush music went –
Almost like a call to come in
To the dark and lament.

But no, I was out for stars:
I would not come in.
I meant not even if asked,
And I hadn't been.

I COULD GIVE ALL TO TIME

To Time it never seems that he is brave
To set himself against the peaks of snow
To lay them level with the running wave,
Nor is he overjoyed when they lie low,
But only grave, contemplative and grave.

What now is inland shall be ocean isle,
Then eddies playing round a sunken reef
Like the curl at the corner of a smile;
And I could share Time's lack of joy or grief
At such a planetary change of style.

I could give all to Time except – except
What I myself have held. But why declare
The things forbidden that while the Customs slept
I have crossed to Safety with? For I am There,
And what I would not part with I have kept.

THE WIND AND THE RAIN

I

That far-off day the leaves in flight
Were letting in the colder light.

A season-ending wind there blew
That, as it did the forest strew,
I leaned on with a singing trust
And let it drive me deathward too.
With breaking step I stabbed the dust,
Yet did not much to shorten stride.
I sang of death – but had I known
The many deaths one must have died
Before he came to meet his own!
Oh, should a child be left unwarned
That any song in which he mourned
Would be as if he prophesied?
It were unworthy of the tongue
To let the half of life alone
And play the good without the ill.
And yet 'twould seem that what is sung
In happy sadness by the young,
Fate has no choice but to fulfill.

II

Flowers in the desert heat
Contrive to bloom
On melted mountain water led by flume
To wet their feet.
But something in it still is incomplete.
Before I thought the wilted to exalt
With water I would see them water-bowed.
I would pick up all ocean less its salt,
And though it were as much as cloud could bear
Would load it onto cloud,
And rolling it inland on roller air,
Would empty it unsparing on the flower
That past its prime lost petals in the flood
(Who cares but for the future of the bud?),

And all the more the mightier the shower
Would run in under it to get my share.

'Tis not enough on roots and in the mouth,
But give me water heavy on the head
In all the passion of a broken drouth.

And there is always more than should be said.

As strong is rain without as wine within,
As magical as sunlight on the skin.

I have been one no dwelling could contain
When there was rain;
But I must forth at dusk, my time of day,
To see to the unburdening of skies.
Rain was the tears adopted by my eyes
That have none left to stay.

THE MOST OF IT

He thought he kept the universe alone;
For all the voice in answer he could wake
Was but the mocking echo of his own
From some tree-hidden cliff across the lake.
Some morning from the boulder-broken beach
He would cry out on life, that what it wants
Is not its own love back in copy speech,
But counter-love, original response.
And nothing ever came of what he cried
Unless it was the embodiment that crashed
In the cliff's talus on the other side,
And then in the far-distant water splashed,
But after a time allowed for it to swim,

Instead of proving human when it neared
And someone else additional to him,
As a great buck it powerfully appeared,
Pushing the crumpled water up ahead,
And landed pouring like a waterfall,
And stumbled through the rocks with horny tread,
And forced the underbrush – and that was all.

THE SUBVERTED FLOWER

She drew back; he was calm:
'It is this that had the power.'
And he lashed his open palm
With the tender-headed flower.
He smiled for her to smile,
But she was either blind
Or willfully unkind.
He eyed her for a while
For a woman and a puzzle.
He flicked and flung the flower,
And another sort of smile
Caught up like fingertips
The corners of his lips
And cracked his ragged muzzle.
She was standing to the waist
In goldenrod and brake,
Her shining hair displaced.
He stretched her either arm
As if she made it ache
To clasp her – not to harm;
As if he could not spare
To touch her neck and hair.
'If this has come to us
And not to me alone —'

So she thought she heard him say;
Though with every word he spoke
His lips were sucked and blown
And the effort made him choke
Like a tiger at a bone.
She had to lean away.
She dared not stir a foot,
Lest movement should provoke
The demon of pursuit
That slumbers in a brute.
It was then her mother's call
From inside the garden wall
Made her steal a look of fear
To see if he could hear
And would pounce to end it all
Before her mother came.
She looked and saw the shame:
A hand hung like a paw,
An arm worked like a saw
As if to be persuasive,
An ingratiating laugh
That cut the snout in half,
An eye become evasive.
A girl could only see
That a flower had marred a man,
But what she could not see
Was that the flower might be
Other than base and fetid:
That the flower had done but part,
And what the flower began
Her own too meager heart
Had terribly completed.
She looked and saw the worst.
And the dog or what it was,
Obeying bestial laws,

A coward save at night,
Turned from the place and ran.
She heard him stumble first
And use his hands in flight.
She heard him bark outright.
And oh, for one so young
The bitter words she spit
Like some tenacious bit
That will not leave the tongue.
She plucked her lips for it,
And still the horror clung.
Her mother wiped the foam
From her chin, picked up her comb,
And drew her backward home.

THE QUEST OF THE PURPLE-FRINGED

I felt the chill of the meadow underfoot,
But the sun overhead;
And snatches of verse and song of scenes like this
I sung or said.

I skirted the margin alders for miles and miles
In a sweeping line.
The day was the day by every flower that blooms,
But I saw no sign.

Yet further I went to be before the scythe,
For the grass was high;
Till I saw the path where the slender fox had come
And gone panting by.

Then at last and following him I found –
In the very hour
When the color flushed to the petals it must have been –
The far-sought flower.

There stood the purple spires with no breath of air
Nor headlong bee
To disturb their perfect poise the livelong day
'Neath the alder tree.

I only knelt and putting the boughs aside
Looked, or at most
Counted them all to the buds in the copse's depth
That were pale as a ghost.

Then I arose and silently wandered home,
And I for one
Said that the fall might come and whirl of leaves,
For summer was done.

THE GIFT OUTRIGHT

The land was ours before we were the land's.
She was our land more than a hundred years
Before we were her people. She was ours
In Massachusetts, in Virginia,
But we were England's, still colonials,
Possessing what we still were unpossessed by,
Possessed by what we now no more possessed.
Something we were withholding made us weak
Until we found out that it was ourselves
We were withholding from our land of living,
And forthwith found salvation in surrender.
Such as we were we gave ourselves outright
(The deed of gift was many deeds of war)
To the land vaguely realizing westward,
But still unstoried, artless, unenhanced,
Such as she was, such as she would become.

OUR HOLD ON THE PLANET

We asked for rain. It didn't flash and roar.
It didn't lose its temper at our demand
And blow a gale. It didn't misunderstand
And give us more than our spokesman bargained for;
And just because we owned to a wish for rain,
Send us a flood and bid us be damned and drown.
It gently threw us a glittering shower down.
And when we had taken that into the roots of grain,
It threw us another and then another still,
Till the spongy soil again was natal wet.
We may doubt the just proportion of good to ill.
There is much in nature against us. But we forget:
Take nature altogether since time began,
Including human nature, in peace and war,
And it must be a little more in favor of man,
Say a fraction of one percent at the very least,
Or our number living wouldn't be steadily more,
Our hold on the planet wouldn't have so increased.

A CONSIDERABLE SPECK

(*Microscopic*)

A speck that would have been beneath my sight
On any but a paper sheet so white
Set off across what I had written there.
And I had idly poised my pen in air
To stop it with a period of ink,
When something strange about it made me think.
This was no dust speck by my breathing blown,
But unmistakably a living mite
With inclinations it could call its own.
It paused as with suspicion of my pen,

And then came racing wildly on again
To where my manuscript was not yet dry;
Then paused again and either drank or smelt –
With loathing, for again it turned to fly.
Plainly with an intelligence I dealt.
It seemed too tiny to have room for feet,
Yet must have had a set of them complete
To express how much it didn't want to die.
It ran with terror and with cunning crept.
It faltered: I could see it hesitate;
Then in the middle of the open sheet
Cower down in desperation to accept
Whatever I accorded it of fate.
I have none of the tenderer-than-thou
Collectivistic regimenting love
With which the modern world is being swept.
But this poor microscopic item now!
Since it was nothing I knew evil of
I let it lie there till I hope it slept.

I have a mind myself and recognize
Mind when I meet with it in any guise.
No one can know how glad I am to find
On any sheet the least display of mind.

A SEMI-REVOLUTION

I advocate a semi-revolution.
The trouble with a total revolution
(Ask any reputable Rosicrucian)
Is that it brings the same class up on top.
Executives of skillful execution
Will therefore plan to go halfway and stop.
Yes, revolutions are the only salves,
But they're one thing that should be done by halves.

A SERIOUS STEP LIGHTLY TAKEN

Between two burrs on the map
Was a hollow-headed snake.
The burrs were hills, the snake was a stream,
And the hollow head was a lake.

And the dot in *front* of a name
Was what should be a town.
And there might be a house we could buy
For only a dollar down.

With two wheels low in the ditch
We left our boiling car
And knocked at the door of a house we found,
And there today we are.

It is turning three hundred years
On our cisatlantic shore
For family after family name.
We'll make it three hundred more

For our name farming here,
Aloof yet not aloof,
Enriching soil and increasing stock,
Repairing fence and roof;

A hundred thousand days
Of front-page paper events,
A half a dozen major wars,
And forty-five presidents.

STEEPLE BUSH

1947

A YOUNG BIRCH

The birch begins to crack its outer sheath
Of baby green and show the white beneath,
As whosoever likes the young and slight
May well have noticed. Soon entirely white
To double day and cut in half the dark
It will stand forth, entirely white in bark,
And nothing but the top a leafy green –
The only native tree that dares to lean,
Relying on its beauty, to the air.
(Less brave perhaps than trusting are the fair.)
And someone reminiscent will recall
How once in cutting brush along the wall
He spared it from the number of the slain,
At first to be no bigger than a cane,
And then no bigger than a fishing pole,
But now at last so obvious a bole
The most efficient help you ever hired
Would know that it was there to be admired,
And zeal would not be thanked that cut it down
When you were reading books or out of town.
It was a thing of beauty and was sent
To live its life out as an ornament.

SOMETHING FOR HOPE

At the present rate it must come to pass,
And that right soon, that the meadowsweet
And steeple bush, not good to eat,
Will have crowded out the edible grass.

Then all there is to do is wait
For maple, birch, and spruce to push
Through meadowsweet and steeple bush
And crowd them out at a similar rate.

No plow among these rocks would pay.
So busy yourself with other things
While the trees put on their wooden rings
And with long-sleeved branches hold their sway.

Then cut down the trees when lumber grown,
And there's your pristine earth all freed
From lovely blooming but wasteful weed
And ready again for the grass to own.

A cycle we'll say of a hundred years.
Thus foresight does it and laissez-faire,
A virtue in which we all may share
Unless a government interferes.

Patience and looking away ahead,
And leaving some things to take their course.
Hope may not nourish a cow or horse,
But *spes alit agricolam* 'tis said.

DIRECTIVE

Back out of all this now too much for us,
Back in a time made simple by the loss
Of detail, burned, dissolved, and broken off
Like graveyard marble sculpture in the weather,
There is a house that is no more a house
Upon a farm that is no more a farm
And in a town that is no more a town.

The road there, if you'll let a guide direct you
Who only has at heart your getting lost,
May seem as if it should have been a quarry –
Great monolithic knees the former town
Long since gave up pretense of keeping covered.
And there's a story in a book about it:
Besides the wear of iron wagon wheels
The ledges show lines ruled southeast-northwest,
The chisel work of an enormous Glacier
That braced his feet against the Arctic Pole.
You must not mind a certain coolness from him
Still said to haunt this side of Panther Mountain.
Nor need you mind the serial ordeal
Of being watched from forty cellar holes
As if by eye pairs out of forty firkins.
As for the woods' excitement over you
That sends light rustle rushes to their leaves,
Charge that to upstart inexperience.
Where were they all not twenty years ago?
They think too much of having shaded out
A few old pecker-fretted apple trees.
Make yourself up a cheering song of how
Someone's road home from work this once was,
Who may be just ahead of you on foot
Or creaking with a buggy load of grain.
The height of the adventure is the height
Of country where two village cultures faded
Into each other. Both of them are lost.
And if you're lost enough to find yourself
By now, pull in your ladder road behind you
And put a sign up CLOSED to all but me.
Then make yourself at home. The only field
Now left's no bigger than a harness gall.
First there's the children's house of make-believe,
Some shattered dishes underneath a pine,

The playthings in the playhouse of the children.
Weep for what little things could make them glad.
Then for the house that is no more a house,
But only a belilaced cellar hole,
Now slowly closing like a dent in dough.
This was no playhouse but a house in earnest.
Your destination and your destiny's
A brook that was the water of the house,
Cold as a spring as yet so near its source,
Too lofty and original to rage.
(We know the valley streams that when aroused
Will leave their tatters hung on barb and thorn.)
I have kept hidden in the instep arch
Of an old cedar at the waterside
A broken drinking goblet like the Grail
Under a spell so the wrong ones can't find it,
So can't get saved, as Saint Mark says they mustn't.
(I stole the goblet from the children's playhouse.)
Here are your waters and your watering place.
Drink and be whole again beyond confusion.

THE MIDDLENESS OF THE ROAD

The road at the top of the rise
Seems to come to an end
And take off into the skies.
So at the distant bend

It seems to go into a wood,
The place of standing still
As long the trees have stood.
But say what Fancy will,

The mineral drops that explode
To drive my ton of car

Are limited to the road.
They deal with near and far,

But have almost nothing to do
With the absolute flight and rest
The universal blue
And local green suggest.

ON BEING IDOLIZED

The wave sucks back and with the last of water
It wraps a wisp of seaweed round my legs,
And with the swift rush of its sandy dregs
So undermines my barefoot stand I totter,
And did I not take steps would be tipped over
Like the ideal of some mistaken lover.

A WISH TO COMPLY

Did I see it go by,
That Millikan mote?
Well, I said that I did.
I made a good try.
But I'm no one to quote.
If I have a defect
It's a wish to comply
And see as I'm bid.
I rather suspect
All I saw was the lid
Going over my eye.
I honestly think
All I saw was a wink.

A CLIFF DWELLING

There sandy seems the golden sky
And golden seems the sandy plain.
No habitation meets the eye
Unless in the horizon rim,
Some halfway up the limestone wall,
That spot of black is not a stain
Or shadow, but a cavern hole,
Where someone used to climb and crawl
To rest from his besetting fears.
I see the callus on his sole,
The disappearing last of him
And of his race starvation slim,
Oh, years ago – ten thousand years.

A CASE FOR JEFFERSON

Harrison loves my country too,
But wants it all made over new.
He's Freudian Viennese by night.
By day he's Marxian Muscovite.
It isn't because he's Russian Jew.
He's Puritan Yankee through and through.
He dotes on Saturday pork and beans.
But his mind is hardly out of his teens:
With him the love of country means
Blowing it all to smithereens
And having it all made over new.

BURSTING RAPTURE

I went to the physician to complain,
The time had been when anyone could turn

To farming for a simple way to earn;
But now 'twas there as elsewhere, any gain
Was made by getting science on the brain;
There was so much more every day to learn,
The discipline of farming was so stern,
It seemed as if I couldn't stand the strain.
But the physician's answer was, 'There, there,
What you complain of, all the nations share.
Their effort is a mounting ecstasy
That when it gets too exquisite to bear
Will find relief in one burst. You shall see.
That's what a certain bomb was sent to be.'

IN THE CLEARING

1962

POD OF THE MILKWEED

Calling all butterflies of every race
From source unknown but from no special place
They ever will return to all their lives,
Because unlike the bees they have no hives,
The milkweed brings up to my very door
The theme of wanton waste in peace and war
As it has never been to me before.
And so it seems a flower's coming out
That should if not be talked then sung about.
The countless wings that from the infinite
Make such a noiseless tumult over it
Do no doubt with their color compensate
For what the drab weed lacks of the ornate.
For drab it is its fondest must admit.
And yes, although it is a flower that flows
With milk and honey, it is bitter milk,
As anyone who ever broke its stem
And dared to taste the wound a little knows.
It tastes as if it might be opiate.
But whatsoever else it may secrete,
Its flowers' distilled honey is so sweet
It makes the butterflies intemperate.
There is no slumber in its juice for them.
One knocks another off from where he clings.
They knock the dyestuff off each other's wings –
With thirst on hunger to the point of lust.
They raise in their intemperance a cloud
Of mingled butterfly and flower dust
That hangs perceptibly above the scene.
In being sweet to these ephemerals
The sober weed has managed to contrive

In our three hundred days and sixty-five
One day too sweet for beings to survive.
Many shall come away as struggle-worn
And spent and dusted off of their regalia,
To which at daybreak they were freshly born,
As after one-of-them's proverbial failure
From having beaten all day long in vain
Against the wrong side of a windowpane.

But waste was of the essence of the scheme.
And all the good they did for man or god
To all those flowers they passionately trod
Was leave as their posterity one pod
With an inheritance of restless dream.
He hangs on upside down with talon feet
In an inquisitive position odd
As any Guatemalan parakeet.
Something eludes him. Is it food to eat?
Or some dim secret of the good of waste?
He almost has it in his talon clutch.
Where have those flowers and butterflies all gone
That science may have staked the future on?
He seems to say the reason why so much
Should come to nothing must be fairly faced.

A CABIN IN THE CLEARING

For Alfred Edwards

MIST. I don't believe the sleepers in this house
Know where they are.

SMOKE. They've been here long enough
To push the woods back from around the house
And part them in the middle with a path.

MIST. And still I doubt if they know where they are.
And I begin to fear they never will.
All they maintain the path for is the comfort
Of visiting with the equally bewildered.
Nearer in plight their neighbors are than distance.

SMOKE. I am the guardian wraith of starlit smoke
That leans out this and that way from their chimney.
I will not have their happiness despaired of.

MIST. No one – not I – would give them up for lost
Simply because they don't know where they are.
I am the damper counterpart of smoke,
That gives off from a garden ground at night
But lifts no higher than a garden grows.
I cotton to their landscape. That's who I am.
I am no further from their fate than you are.

SMOKE. They must by now have learned the native tongue.
Why don't they ask the Red Man where they are?

MIST. They often do, and none the wiser for it.
So do they also ask philosophers
Who come to look in on them from the pulpit.
They will ask anyone there is to ask –
In the fond faith accumulated fact
Will of itself take fire and light the world up.
Learning has been a part of their religion.

SMOKE. If the day ever comes when they know who
They are, they may know better where they are.
But who they are is too much to believe –
Either for them or the onlooking world.
They are too sudden to be credible.

MIST. Listen, they murmur talking in the dark
On what should be their daylong theme continued.
Putting the lamp out has not put their thought out.

Let us pretend the dewdrops from the eaves
Are you and I eavesdropping on their unrest –
A mist and smoke eavesdropping on a haze –
And see if we can tell the bass from the soprano.

Than smoke and mist who better could appraise
The kindred spirit of an inner haze?

ESCAPIST – NEVER

He is no fugitive – escaped, escaping.
No one has seen him stumble looking back.
His fear is not behind him but beside him
On either hand to make his course perhaps
A crooked straightness yet no less a straightness.
He runs face forward. He is a pursuer.
He seeks a seeker who in his turn seeks
Another still, lost far into the distance.
Any who seek him seek in him the seeker.
His life is a pursuit of a pursuit forever.
It is the future that creates his present.
All is an interminable chain of longing.

FOR JOHN F. KENNEDY HIS INAUGURATION

Gift outright of 'The Gift Outright'
(With some preliminary history in rhyme)

Summoning artists to participate
In the august occasions of the state
Seems something artists ought to celebrate.
Today is for my cause a day of days.
And his be poetry's old-fashioned praise

Who was the first to think of such a thing.
This verse that in acknowledgment I bring
Goes back to the beginning of the end
Of what had been for centuries the trend;
A turning point in modern history.
Colonial had been the thing to be
As long as the great issue was to see
What country'd be the one to dominate
By character, by tongue, by native trait,
The new world Christopher Columbus found.
The French, the Spanish, and the Dutch were downed
And counted out. Heroic deeds were done.
Elizabeth the First and England won.
Now came on a new order of the ages
That in the Latin of our founding sages
(Is it not written on the dollar bill
We carry in our purse and pocket still?)
God nodded His approval of as good.
So much those heroes knew and understood –
I mean the great four, Washington,
John Adams, Jefferson, and Madison –
So much they knew as consecrated seers
They must have seen ahead what now appears:
They would bring empires down about our ears
And by the example of our Declaration
Make everybody want to be a nation.
And this is no aristocratic joke
At the expense of negligible folk.
We see how seriously the races swarm
In their attempts at sovereignty and form.
They are our wards we think to some extent
For the time being and with their consent,
To teach them how Democracy is meant.
'New order of the ages' did we say?
If it looks none too orderly today,

'Tis a confusion it was ours to start
So in it have to take courageous part.
No one of honest feeling would approve
A ruler who pretended not to love
A turbulence he had the better of.
Everyone knows the glory of the twain
Who gave America the aeroplane
To ride the whirlwind and the hurricane.
Some poor fool has been saying in his heart
Glory is out of date in life and art.
Our venture in revolution and outlawry
Has justified itself in freedom's story
Right down to now in glory upon glory.
Come fresh from an election like the last,
The greatest vote a people ever cast,
So close yet sure to be abided by,
It is no miracle our mood is high.
Courage is in the air in bracing whiffs
Better than all the stalemate an's and ifs.
There was the book of profile tales declaring
For the emboldened politicians daring
To break with followers when in the wrong,
A healthy independence of the throng,
A democratic form of right divine
To rule first answerable to high design.
There is a call to life a little sterner,
And braver for the earner, learner, yearner.
Less criticism of the field and court
And more preoccupation with the sport.
It makes the prophet in us all presage
The glory of a next Augustan age
Of a power leading from its strength and pride,
Of young ambition eager to be tried,
Firm in our free beliefs without dismay,
In any game the nations want to play.

A golden age of poetry and power
Of which this noonday's the beginning hour.

THE DRAFT HORSE

With a lantern that wouldn't burn
In too frail a buggy we drove
Behind too heavy a horse
Through a pitch-dark limitless grove.

And a man came out of the trees
And took our horse by the head
And reaching back to his ribs
Deliberately stabbed him dead.

The ponderous beast went down
With a crack of a broken shaft.
And the night drew through the trees
In one long invidious draft.

The most unquestioning pair
That ever accepted fate
And the least disposed to ascribe
Any more than we had to to hate,

We assumed that the man himself
Or someone he had to obey
Wanted us to get down
And walk the rest of the way.

ENDS

Loud talk in the overlighted house
That made us stumble past.

Oh, there had once been night the first,
But this was night the last.

Of all the things he might have said,
Sincere or insincere,
He never said she wasn't young,
And hadn't been his dear.

Oh, some as soon would throw it all
As throw a part away.
And some will say all sorts of things,
But some mean what they say.

PERIL OF HOPE

It is right in there
Betwixt and between
The orchard bare
And the orchard green,

When the boughs are right
In a flowery burst
Of pink and white,
That we fear the worst.

For there's not a clime
But at any cost
Will take that time
For a night of frost.

LINES WRITTEN IN DEJECTION ON THE EVE OF GREAT SUCCESS

I once had a cow that jumped over the moon,
Not onto the moon but over.
I don't know what made her so lunar a loon;
All she'd been having was clover.

That was back in the days of my godmother Goose.
But though we are goosier now,
And all tanked up with mineral juice,
We haven't caught up with my cow.

POSTSCRIPT

But if over the moon I had wanted to go
And had caught my cow by the tail,
I'll bet she'd have made a melodious low
And put her foot in the pail;

Than which there is no indignity worse.
A cow did that once to a fellow
Who rose from the milking stool with a curse
And cried, 'I'll larn you to bellow.'

He couldn't lay hands on a pitchfork to hit her
Or give her a stab of the tine,
So he leapt on her hairy back and bit her
Clear into her marrow spine.

No doubt she would have preferred the fork.
She let out a howl of rage
That was heard as far away as New York
And made the papers' front page.

He answered her back, 'Well, who begun it?'
That's what at the end of a war
We always say – not who won it,
Or what it was foughten for.

ON BEING CHOSEN POET OF VERMONT

Breathes there a bard who isn't moved
When he finds his verse is understood
And not entirely disapproved
By his country and his neighborhood?

A MASQUE OF REASON

1945

A fair oasis in the purest desert.
A man sits leaning back against a palm.
His wife lies by him looking at the sky.

MAN. You're not asleep?

WIFE. No, I can hear you. Why?

MAN. I said the incense tree's on fire again.

WIFE. You mean the Burning Bush?

MAN. The Christmas Tree.

WIFE. I shouldn't be surprised.

MAN. The strangest light!

WIFE. There's a strange light on everything today.

MAN. The myrrh tree gives it. Smell the rosin burning?
The ornaments the Greek artificers
Made for the Emperor Alexius,
The Star of Bethlehem, the pomegranates,
The birds, seem all on fire with Paradise.
And hark, the gold enameled nightingales
Are singing. Yes, and look, the Tree is troubled.
Someone's caught in the branches.

WIFE. So there is.
He can't get out.

MAN. He's loose! He's out!

WIFE. It's God.
I'd know Him by Blake's picture anywhere.
Now what's He doing?

MAN. Pitching throne, I guess,
Here by our atoll.

WIFE. Something Byzantine.

(The throne's a plywood flat, prefabricated,
That God pulls lightly upright on its hinges
And stands beside, supporting it in place.)

Perhaps for an Olympic Tournament,
Or Court of Love.

MAN. More likely Royal Court –
Or Court of Law, and this is Judgment Day.
I trust it is. Here's where I lay aside
My varying opinion of myself
And come to rest in an official verdict.
Suffer yourself to be admired, my love,
As Waller says.

WIFE. Or not admired. Go over
And speak to Him before the others come.
Tell Him He may remember you: you're Job.

GOD. Oh, I remember well: you're Job, my Patient.
How are you now? I trust you're quite recovered,
And feel no ill effects from what I gave you.

JOB. Gave me in truth: I like the frank admission.
I am a name for being put upon.
But, yes, I'm fine, except for now and then
A reminiscent twinge of rheumatism.
The letup's heavenly. You perhaps will tell us
If that is all there is to be of Heaven,
Escape from so great pains of life on earth
It gives a sense of letup calculated
To last a fellow to Eternity.

GOD. Yes, by and by. But first a larger matter.
I've had you on my mind a thousand years
To thank you someday for the way you helped me

Establish once for all the principle
There's no connection man can reason out
Between his just deserts and what he gets.
Virtue may fail and wickedness succeed.
'Twas a great demonstration we put on.
I should have spoken sooner had I found
The word I wanted. You would have supposed
One who in the beginning *was* the Word
Would be in a position to command it.
I have to wait for words like anyone.
Too long I've owed you this apology
For the apparently unmeaning sorrow
You were afflicted with in those old days.
But it was of the essence of the trial
You shouldn't understand it at the time.
It had to seem unmeaning to have meaning.
And it came out all right. I have no doubt
You realize by now the part you played
To stultify the Deuteronomist
And change the tenor of religious thought.
My thanks are to you for releasing me
From moral bondage to the human race.
The only free will there at first was man's,
Who could do good or evil as he chose.
I had no choice but I must follow him
With forfeits and rewards he understood –
Unless I liked to suffer loss of worship.
I had to prosper good and punish evil.
You changed all that. You set me free to reign.
You are the Emancipator of your God,
And as such I promote you to a saint.

JOB. You hear Him, Thyatira: we're a saint.
Salvation in our case is retroactive.
We're saved, we're saved, whatever else it means.

JOB'S WIFE. Well, after all these years!

JOB. This is my wife.

JOB'S WIFE. If You're the deity I assume You are
(I'd know You by Blake's picture anywhere) –

GOD. The best, I'm told, I ever have had taken.

JOB'S WIFE. – I have a protest I would lodge with You.
I want to ask You if it stands to reason
That women prophets should be burned as witches,
Whereas men prophets are received with honor.

JOB. Except in their own country, Thyatira.

GOD. You're not a witch?

JOB'S WIFE. No.

GOD. Have you ever been one?

JOB. Sometimes she thinks she has and gets herself
Worked up about it. But she really hasn't –
Not in the sense of having to my knowledge
Predicted anything that came to pass.

JOB'S WIFE. The Witch of Endor was a friend of mine.

GOD. You wouldn't say she fared so very badly.
I noticed when she called up Samuel
His spirit had to come. Apparently
A witch was stronger than a prophet there.

JOB'S WIFE. But she was burned for witchcraft.

GOD. That is not
Of record in my Note Book.

JOB'S WIFE. Well, she was.
And I should like to know the reason why.

GOD. There you go asking for the very thing
We've just agreed I didn't have to give. –

(The throne collapses. But He picks it up
And this time locks it up and leaves it.)

Where has she been the last half hour or so?
She wants to know why there is still injustice.
I answer flatly: That's the way it is,
And bid my will avouch it like Macbeth.
We may as well go back to the beginning
And look for justice in the case of Segub.

JOB. Oh, Lord, let's not go *back* to anything.

GOD. Because your wife's past won't bear looking into? –
In our great moment what did you do, Madam?
What did you try to make your husband say?

JOB'S WIFE. No, let's not live things over. I don't care.
I stood by Job. I may have turned on You.
Job scratched his boils and tried to think what he
Had done or not done to or for the poor.
The test is always how we treat the poor.
It's time the poor were treated by the state
In some way not so penal as the poorhouse.
That's one thing more to put on Your agenda.
Job hadn't done a thing, poor innocent.
I told him not to scratch: it made it worse.
If I said once I said a thousand times,
Don't scratch! And when, as rotten as his skin,
His tents blew all to pieces, I picked up
Enough to build him every night a pup tent
Around him so it wouldn't touch and hurt him.
I did my wifely duty. I should tremble!
All You can seem to do is lose Your temper
When reason-hungry mortals ask for reasons.

Of course, in the abstract high singular
There isn't any universal reason;
And no one but a man would think there was.
You don't catch women trying to be Plato.
Still there must be lots of unsystematic
Stray scraps of palliative reason
It wouldn't hurt You to vouchsafe the faithful.
You thought it was agreed You needn't give them.
You thought to suit Yourself. I've not agreed
To anything with anyone.

JOB. There, there,
You go to sleep. God must await events,
As well as words.

JOB'S WIFE. I'm serious. God's had
Aeons of time and still it's mostly women
Get burned for prophecy, men almost never.

JOB. God needs time just as much as you or I
To get things done. Reformers fail to see that. –
She'll go to sleep. Nothing keeps her awake
But physical activity, I find.
Try to read to her and she drops right off.

GOD. She's beautiful.

JOB. Yes, she was just remarking
She now felt younger by a thousand years
Than the day she was born.

GOD. That's about right,
I should have said. You got your age reversed
When time was found to be a space dimension
That could, like any space, be turned around in?

JOB. Yes, both of us: we saw to that at once.
But, God, I have a question too to raise.

(My wife gets in ahead of me with hers.)
I need some help about this reason problem
Before I am too late to be got right
As to what reasons I agree to waive.
I'm apt to string along with Thyatira.
God knows – or rather, You know (God forgive me)
I waived the reason for my ordeal – but –
I have a question even there to ask –
In confidence. There's no one here but her,
And she's a woman: she's not interested
In general ideas and principles.

GOD. What are her interests, Job?

JOB. Witch-women's rights.
Humor her there or she will be confirmed
In her suspicion You're no feminist.
You have it in for women, she believes.
Kipling invokes You as Lord God of Hosts.
She'd like to know how You would take a prayer
That started off Lord God of Hostesses.

GOD. I'm charmed with her.

JOB. Yes, I could see You were.
But to my question. I am much impressed
With what You say we have established,
Between us, You and I.

GOD. I make you see?
It would be too bad if Columbus-like
You failed to see the worth of your achievement.

JOB. You call it mine.

GOD. We groped it out together.
Any originality it showed
I give you credit for. My forte is truth,

Or metaphysics, long the world's reproach
For standing still in one place true forever;
While science goes self-superseding on.
Look at how far we've left the current science
Of Genesis behind. The wisdom there, though,
Is just as good as when I uttered it.
Still, novelty has doubtless an attraction.

JOB. So it's important who first thinks of things?

GOD. I'm a great stickler for the author's name.
By proper names I find I do my thinking.

JOB'S WIFE. God, who invented earth?

JOB. What, still awake?

GOD. Any originality it showed
Was of the Devil. He invented Hell,
False premises that are the original
Of all originality, the sin
That felled the angels, Wolsey should have said.
As for the earth, we groped that out together,
Much as your husband, Job, and I together
Found out the discipline man needed most
Was to learn his submission to unreason;
And that for man's own sake as well as mine,
So he won't find it hard to take his orders
From his inferiors in intelligence
In peace and war – especially in war.

JOB. So he won't find it hard to take his war.

GOD. You have the idea. There's not much I can tell you.

JOB. All very splendid. I am flattered proud
To have been in on anything with You.
'Twas a great demonstration if You say so.
Though incidentally I sometimes wonder
Why it had had to be at my expense.

GOD. It had to be at somebody's expense.
Society can never think things out:
It has to see them acted out by actors,
Devoted actors at a sacrifice –
The ablest actors I can lay my hands on.
Is that your answer?

JOB. No, for I have yet
To ask my question. We disparage reason.
But all the time it's what we're most concerned with.
There's will as motor and there's will as brakes.
Reason is, I suppose, the steering gear.
The will as brakes can't stop the will as motor
For very long. We're plainly made to go.
We're going anyway and may as well
Have some say as to where we're headed for;
Just as we will be talking anyway
And may as well throw in a little sense.
Let's do so now. Because I let You off
From telling me Your reason, don't assume
I thought You had none. Somewhere back
I knew You had one. But this isn't it
You're giving me. You say we groped this out.
But if You will forgive me the irreverence,
It sounds to me as if You thought it out,
And took Your time to it. It seems to me
An afterthought, a long-long-after-thought.
I'd give more for one least beforehand reason
Than all the justifying ex-post-facto
Excuses trumped up by You for theologists.
The front of being answerable to no one
I'm with You in maintaining to the public.
But, Lord, we showed them what. The audience
Has all gone home to bed. The play's played out.
Come, after all these years – to satisfy me.

I'm curious. And I'm a grown-up man:
I'm not a child for You to put me off
And tantalize me with another 'Oh, because.'
You'd be the last to want me to believe
All Your effects were merely lucky blunders.
That would be unbelief and atheism.
The artist in me cries out for design.
Such devilish ingenuity of torture
Did seem unlike You, and I tried to think
The reason might have been some other person's.
But there is nothing You are not behind.
I did not ask then, but it seems as if
Now after all these years You might indulge me.
Why did You hurt me so? I am reduced
To asking flatly for the reason – outright.

GOD. I'd tell you, Job —

JOB. All right, don't tell me, then,
If you don't want to. I don't want to know.
But what is all this secrecy about?
I fail to see what fun, what satisfaction
A God can find in laughing at how badly
Men fumble at the possibilities
When left to guess forever for themselves.
The chances are when there's so much pretense
Of metaphysical profundity
The obscurity's a fraud to cover nothing.
I've come to think no so-called hidden value's
Worth going after. Get down into things,
It will be found there's no more given there
Than on the surface. If there ever was,
The crypt was long since rifled by the Greeks.
We don't know where we are, or who we are.
We don't know one another; don't know You;
Don't know what time it is. We don't know, don't we?

Who says we don't? Who got up these misgivings?
Oh, we know well enough to go ahead with.
I mean we seem to know enough to act on.
It comes down to a doubt about the wisdom
Of having children – after having had them,
So there is nothing we can do about it
But warn the children they perhaps should have none.
You could end this by simply coming out
And saying plainly and unequivocally
Whether there's any part of man immortal.
Yet You don't speak. Let fools bemuse themselves
By being baffled for the sake of being.
I'm sick of the whole artificial puzzle.

JOB'S WIFE. You won't get any answers out of God.

GOD. My kingdom, what an outbreak!

JOB'S WIFE. Job is right.
Your kingdom, yes, Your kingdom come on earth.
Pray tell me what does that mean? Anything?
Perhaps that earth is going to crack someday
Like a big egg and hatch a heaven out
Of all the dead and buried from their graves.
One simple little statement from the throne
Would put an end to such fantastic nonsense;
And, too, take care of twenty of the four
And twenty freedoms on the party docket.
Or is it only four? My extra twenty
Are freedoms from the need of asking questions.
(I hope You know the game called twenty questions.)
For instance, is there such a thing as Progress?
Job says there's no such thing as Earth's becoming
An easier place for man to save his soul in.
Except as a hard place to save his soul in,
A trial ground where he can try himself

And find out whether he is any good,
It would be meaningless. It might as well
Be Heaven at once and have it over with.

GOD. Two pitching on like this tend to confuse me.
One at a time, please. I will answer Job first.
I'm going to tell Job why I tortured him,
And trust it won't be adding to the torture.
I was just showing off to the Devil, Job,
As is set forth in Chapters One and Two.
(*Job takes a few steps pacing.*) Do you mind?
(*God eyes him anxiously.*)

JOB. No. No, I mustn't.
'Twas human of You. I expected more
Than I could understand and what I get
Is almost less than I can understand.
But I don't mind. Let's leave it as it stood.
The point was it was none of my concern.
I stick to that. But talk about confusion! –
How is that for a mix-up, Thyatira? –
Yet I suppose what seems to us confusion
Is not confusion, but the form of forms,
The serpent's tail stuck down the serpent's throat,
Which is the symbol of eternity
And also of the way all things come round,
Or of how rays return upon themselves,
To quote the greatest Western poem yet.
Though I hold rays deteriorate to nothing:
First white, then red, then ultrared, then out.

GOD. Job, you must understand my provocation.
The tempter comes to me and I am tempted.
I'd had about enough of his derision
Of what I valued most in human nature.
He thinks he's smart. He thinks he can convince me

It is no different with my followers
From what it is with his. Both serve for pay.
Disinterestedness never did exist,
And if it did, it wouldn't be a virtue.
Neither would fairness. You have heard the doctrine.
It's on the increase. He could count on no one:
That was his lookout. I could count on you.
I wanted him forced to acknowledge so much.
I gave you over to him, but with safeguards.
I took care of you. And before you died
I trust I made it clear I took your side
Against your comforters in their contention
You must be wicked to deserve such pain.
That's Browning and sheer Chapel Non-conformism.

JOB. God, please, enough for now. I'm in no mood
For more excuses.

GOD. What I mean to say:
Your comforters were wrong.

JOB. Oh, that committee!

GOD. I saw you had no fondness for committees.
Next time you find yourself pressed onto one
For the revision of the Book of Prayer
Put that in if it isn't in already:
Deliver us from committees. 'Twill remind me.
I would do anything for you in reason.

JOB. Yes, yes.

GOD. You don't seem satisfied.

JOB. I am.

GOD. You're pensive.

JOB. Oh, I'm thinking of the Devil.

You must remember he was in on this.
We can't leave him out.

GOD. No. No, we don't need to.
We're too well off.

JOB. Someday we three should have
A good old get-together celebration.

GOD. Why not right now?

JOB. We can't without the Devil.

GOD. The Devil's never very far away.
He too is pretty circumambient.
He has but to appear. He'll come for me,
Precipitated from the desert air. –
Show yourself, son. – I'll get back on my throne
For this I think. I find it always best
To be upon my dignity with him.

(The Devil enters like a sapphire wasp
That flickers mica wings. He lifts a hand
To brush away a disrespectful smile.
Job's wife sits up.)

JOB'S WIFE. Well, if we aren't all here,
Including me, the only Dramatis
Personae needed to enact the problem.

JOB. We've waked her up.

JOB'S WIFE. I haven't been asleep.
I've heard what you were saying – every word.

JOB. What did we say?

JOB'S WIFE. You said the Devil's in it.

JOB. She always claims she hasn't been asleep. –
And what else did we say?

JOB'S WIFE. Well, what led up –
Something about – (*The three men laugh.*)
– The Devil's being God's best inspiration.

JOB. Good, pretty good.

JOB'S WIFE. Wait till I get my Kodak. –
Would you two please draw in a little closer?
No – no, that's not a smile there. That's a grin.
Satan, what ails you? Where's the famous tongue,
Thou onetime Prince of Conversationists?
This is polite society you're in,
Where good and bad are mingled every which way,
And ears are lent to any sophistry
Just as if nothing mattered but our manners.
You look as if you either hoped or feared
You were more guilty of mischief than you are.
Nothing has been brought out that for my part
I'm not prepared for or that Job himself
Won't find a formula for taking care of.

SATAN. Like the one Milton found to fool himself
About his blindness.

JOB'S WIFE. Oh, he speaks! He *can* speak!
That strain again! Give me excess of it!
As dulcet as a pagan temple gong!
He's twitting us. – Oh, by the way, you haven't
By any chance a Lady Apple on you?
I saw a boxful in the Christmas market.
How I should prize one personally from you.

GOD. Don't *you* twit. He's unhappy. Church neglect
And figurative use have pretty well
Reduced him to a shadow of himself.

JOB'S WIFE. *That* explains why he's so diaphanous
And easy to see through. But where's he off to?

I thought there were to be festivities
Of some kind. We could have charades.

GOD. He has his business he must be about.
Job mentioned him, and so I brought him in,
More to give his reality its due
Than anything.

JOB'S WIFE. He's very real to me
And always will be. – Please don't go. Stay, stay
But to the evensong, and having played
Together we will go with you along.
There are who won't have had enough of you
If you go now. – Look how he takes no steps!
He isn't really going, yet he's leaving.

JOB. (*Who has been standing dazed with new ideas*)
He's on that tendency that like the Gulf Stream,
Only of sand, not water, runs through here.
It has a rate distinctly different
From the surrounding desert; just today
I stumbled over it and got tripped up.

JOB'S WIFE. Oh, yes, that tendency! – Oh, do come off it.
Don't let it carry you away. I hate
A tendency. The minute you get on one
It seems to start right off accelerating.
Here, take my hand.

(*He takes it and alights*
In three quick steps as off an escalator.
The tendency, a long, long narrow strip
Of middle-aisle church carpet, sisal hemp,
Is worked by hands invisible, offstage.)

I want you in my group beside the throne –
Must have you. There, that's just the right arrangement.
Now someone can light up the Burning Bush

And turn the gold enameled artificial birds on.
I recognize them. Greek artificers
Devised them for Alexius Comnenus.
They won't show in the picture. That's too bad.
Neither will I show. That's too bad moreover.
Now if you three have settled anything
You'd as well smile as frown on the occasion.

(*Here endeth Chapter Forty-three of Job.*)

A MASQUE OF MERCY

1947

A bookstore late at night. The Keeper's wife
Pulls down the window curtain on the door
And locks the door. One customer, locked in,
Stays talking with the Keeper at a showcase.
The Keeper's wife has hardly turned away
Before the door's so violently tried
It makes her move as if to reinforce it.

JESSE BEL. You can't come in! (*Knock, knock*) The store is closed!

PAUL. Late, late, too late, you cannot enter now.

JESSE BEL. We can't be always selling people things.
He doesn't go.

KEEPER. You needn't be so stern.
Open enough to find out who it is.

JESSE BEL. Keeper, you come and see. Or you come, Paul.
Our second second-childhood case tonight.
Where do these senile runaways escape from?
Wretchedness in a stranger frightens me
More than it touches me.

PAUL. You may come in.

FUGITIVE. (*Entering hatless in a whirl of snow*)
God's after me!

JESSE BEL. You mean the Devil is.

FUGITIVE. No, God.

JESSE BEL. I never heard of such a thing.

FUGITIVE. Haven't you heard of Thompson's 'Hound of Heaven'?

PAUL. 'I fled Him, down the nights and down the days;
I fled Him, down the arches of the years.'

KEEPER. This is a bookstore – not a sanctuary.

JESSE BEL. I thought you just now said it was a gift shop.

KEEPER. Don't you be bitter about it. I'm not bitter.

FUGITIVE. Well, I could use a book.

KEEPER. What book?

FUGITIVE. A Bible.

KEEPER. To find out how to get away from God?
Which is what people use it for too often –
And why we wouldn't have one in the store.
We don't believe the common man should read it.
Let him seek his religion in the Church.

JESSE BEL. Keeper, be still. – Pay no attention to him.
He's being a religious snob for fun.
The name his mother gave him is to blame
For Keeper's levity: My Brother's Keeper.
She didn't do it to him to be quaint,
But out of politics. She told me so.
She was left over from the Brook Farm venture.

KEEPER. Why is God after you? – to save your soul?

FUGITIVE. No, make me prophesy.

JESSE BEL. And – you – just – won't?

FUGITIVE. Haven't you noticed anything (hear that!)
Since I came in?

KEEPER. Hear what? That army truck?

FUGITIVE. Look, I don't need the Bible to consult.
I just thought if you had a copy handy,

I could point out my sort of passport in it.
There is a story you may have forgotten
About a whale.

KEEPER. Oh, you mean *Moby Dick*
By Rockwell Kent that everybody's reading.
Trust me to help you find the book you want.

JESSE BEL. Keeper, be still. He knows what book he wants.
He said the Bible.

FUGITIVE. I should hate to scare you
With the suspicion at this hour of night
That I might be a confidence impostor.
I'm Jonas Dove – if that is any help.

PAUL. Which is the same as saying Jonah, Jonah –
Ah, Jonah, Jonah – twice – reproachfully.

FUGITIVE. Spare me the setting of my fate to music.
How did you know that way to break my heart?
Who are you?

PAUL. Who are *you*?

JONAH. I think you know,
You seem so ready at translating names.
Unless I'm much mistaken in myself
This is the seventh time I have been sent
To prophesy against the city evil.

KEEPER. What have you got against the city?

JONAH. *He* knows.
We have enough against it, haven't we?
Cursed be the era that congested it.

KEEPER. Come, come, you talk like an agrarian.
The city is all right. To live in one
Is to be civilized, stay up and read

Or sing and dance all night and see sunrise
By waiting up instead of getting up.
The country's only useful as a place
To rest at times from being civilized.
You take us two, we're losers in this store,
So losers in the city, but we're game:
We don't go back on grapes we couldn't reach.
We blame ourselves. We're good sports, aren't we, Bel?

JESSE BEL. I'm not a sport and don't pretend I am one. –
It's only fair to Keeper to inform you
His favorite reading is seed catalogues.
When he gets too agrarian for me
I take to drink – at least I take *a* drink.

(*She has her own glass in a vacant chair.*)

PAUL. She'll take to drink and see how we like that.

KEEPER. Bel is a solitary social drinker.
She doesn't mind not offering a drink
To anyone around when she is drinking.

JESSE BEL. We're poor – that's why. My man can't earn a living.

KEEPER. Is it just any city you're against?

JONAH. Yes, but New York will do as an example.

KEEPER. Well, you're as good as in New York this minute –
Or bad as in New York.

JONAH. I know I am.
That was where my engagement was to speak
This very night. I had the hall all hired,
The audience assembled. There I was
Behind the scenes, ordained and advertised
To prophesy, and full of prophecy,

Yet could not bring myself to say a word.
I left light shining on an empty stage
And fled to you. But you receive me not.

KEEPER. Yes, we do too, with sympathy, my friend.
Your righteous indignation fizzled out,
Or else you were afraid of being mobbed
If what you had to say was disagreeable.

JESSE BEL. Your courage failed. The saddest thing in life
Is that the best thing in it should be courage.
Them is my sentiments, and, Mr Flood,
Since you propose it, I believe I will.

JONAH. Please, someone understand.

PAUL. I understand.

JONAH. These others don't.

PAUL. You don't yourself entirely.

JONAH. What don't I understand? It's easy enough.
I'm in the Bible, all done out in story.
I've lost my faith in God to carry out
The threats He makes against the city evil.
I can't trust God to be unmerciful.

KEEPER. You've lost your faith in God? How wicked of you.

JESSE BEL. You naughty kitten, you shall have no pie.

PAUL. Keeper's the kind of Unitarian
Who having by elimination got
From many gods to Three, and Three to One,
Thinks why not taper off to none at all,
Except as father putative to sort of
Legitimize the brotherhood of man,
So we can hang together in a strike.

KEEPER. Now we are hearing from the Exegete.

You don't know Paul: he's in the Bible too.
He is the fellow who theologized
Christ almost out of Christianity.
Look out for him.

PAUL. 'Look out for me' is right.
I'm going to tell you something, Jonas Dove.
I'm going to take the nonsense out of you
And give you rest, poor Wandering Jew.

JONAH. I'm not
The Wandering Jew – I'm who I say I am,
A Prophet with the Bible for credentials.

PAUL. I never said you weren't. I recognized you.
You are the universal fugitive –
Escapist, as we say – though you are not
Running away from Him you think you are,
But from His mercy-justice contradiction.
Mercy and justice are a contradiction.
But here's where your evasion has an end.
I have to tell you something that will spoil
Indulgence in your form of melancholy
Once and for all. I'm going to make you see
How relatively little justice matters.

JONAH. I see what you are up to: robbing me
Of my incentive – canceling my mission.

PAUL. I am empowered to excuse you from it.

JONAH. You! Who are you? I asked you once before.

JESSE BEL. He is our analyst.

JONAH. Your analyst?

KEEPER. Who keeps our bookstore annals.

JESSE BEL. Stop it, Keeper. –

An analyst's the latest thing in doctors.
He's mine. That's what he is (you asked) – my doctor.
I'm sick.

JONAH. Of what?

JESSE BEL. Oh, everything, I guess.
The doctors say the trouble with me is
I'm not in love. I didn't love the doctor
I had before. That's why I changed to Paul –
To try another.

PAUL. Jesse Bel's a girl
Whose cure will lie in getting her idea
Of the word love corrected. She got off
To a bad start it seems in the wrong school
Of therapy.

JESSE BEL. I don't love Paul – as yet.

JONAH. How about loving God?

JESSE BEL. You make me shrug. –
And I don't love you either, do I, Keeper?

KEEPER. Don't lay your hand on me to say it, shameless.
Let me alone.

JESSE BEL. I'm sick. Joe's sick. The world's sick.
I'll take to drink – at least I'll take *a* drink.

JONAH. My name's not Joe. I don't like what she says.
It's Greenwich Village cocktail-party talk –
Big-city talk. I'm getting out of here.
'I'm – bound – away!' (*He quotes it to the tune.*)

PAUL. Oh, no, you're not. You're staying here tonight. –
You locked the door, Bel. Let me have the key.

(*He goes and takes it from the door himself.*)

JONAH. Then I'm a prisoner?

PAUL. You are tonight.
We take it you were sent in here for help.
And help you're going to get.

JONAH. I'll break your door down.
Always the same when I set out in flight.
I take the first boat. God puts up a storm
That someone in the crew connects with me.
The sailors throw me overboard for luck,
Or, as you might say, throw me to the whale –
For me to disagree with him and get spit out
Right back in the same trouble I was in.
You're modern; so the whale you throw me to
Will be some soulless lunatic asylum –
For me to disagree with any science
There may be there and get spit out again.

JESSE BEL. You poor, poor swallowable little man.

PAUL. If you would take the hands out of your hair
And calm yourself. Be sane! I hereby hold
Your forearms in the figure of a cross
The way it rested two points on the ground
At every station but the final one.

JONAH. What good is that?

PAUL. I'll make you see what good.

JONAH. I *am* sick, as she says. Nothing exhausts me
Like working myself up to prophesy
And then not prophesying. (*He sits down.*)

JESSE BEL. Can you interpret dreams? I dreamed last night
Someone took curved nail-scissors and snipped off
My eyelids so I couldn't shut my eyes
To anything that happened anymore.

JONAH. She's had some loss she can't accept from God –
Is that it? Some Utopian belief –
Or child, and this is motherly resentment?

JESSE BEL. You look so sleepless. – If he'd promise us
To go straight home, we wouldn't keep him, would we? –
Where are you staying – anywhere in town?

JONAH. Under the bandstand in Suburban Park.

JESSE BEL. Why, what a story. At this time of year
There's not a footprint to it in the snow.

PAUL. Jonah, I'm glad, not sad, to hear you say
You can't trust God to be unmerciful.
There you have the beginning of all wisdom.

KEEPER. One minute, may I, Paul? – before we leave
Religion for these philosophic matters.
That's the right style of coat for prophecy
You're sporting there. I'll bet you're good at it.
Shall it be told we had a prophet captive
And let him get off without prophesying?
Let's have some prophecy. What form of ruin
(For ruin I assume was what it was)
Had you in mind to visit on the city,
Rebellion, pestilence, invasion?

JONAH. Earthquake
Was what I thought of.

KEEPER. Have you any grounds,
Or undergrounds, for confidence in earthquake?

JONAH. It's good geology – the Funday Fault,
A fracture in the rocks beneath New York
That only needs a finger touch from God
To spring it like a deadfall and the fault
In nature would wipe out all human fault.

(*He stops to listen.*) That's a mighty storm,
And we are shaken. But it isn't earthquake.
Another possibility I thought of –

(He stops to listen and his unspoken thought,
Projected from the lantern of his eyes,
Is thrown in script, as at Belshazzar's feast,
On the blank curtain on the outer door.)

– Was Babel: everyone developing
A language of his own to write his book in,
And one to cap the climax by combining
All language in a one-man tongue-confusion.

(He starts to speak, but stops again to listen.
The writing on the screen must change too fast
For any but the rapidest eye readers.)

Suspicion of the income-tax returns,
A question who was getting the most out
Of business, might increase into a madness.
The mob might hold a man up in the streets
And tear his clothes off to examine him
To find if there were pockets in his skin,
As in a smuggler's at the diamond fields,
Where he was hoarding more than they enjoyed.

PAUL. We can all see what's passing in your mind.
(I won't have Keeper calling it religion.)
It's a hard case. It's got so prophecy
Is a disease of your imagination.
You're so lost in the virtuosity
Of getting up good ruins, you've forgotten
What the sins are men ought to perish for.

JONAH. You wrong me.

KEEPER. Well then, name a single sin.

JONAH. Another possibility I thought of –

JESSE BEL. There he goes off into another trance.

KEEPER. You stick to earthquake, you have something there –
Something we'll know we're getting when we get it.

PAUL. (*Taking a walk off down the store distressed*)
Keeper, I'll turn on you if you keep on.

KEEPER. If I were in your place, though, Mr Prophet,
I'd *want* to be more certain I was called,
Before I undertook so delicate
A mission as to have to tell New York
'Twas in for an old-fashioned shaking down
Like the one Joshua gave Jericho.
You wouldn't want the night clubs laughing at you.

JESSE BEL. Or *The New Yorker*.

KEEPER. When was the last time
You heard from God – I mean had orders from Him?

JONAH. I'm hearing from Him now, did you but notice.
Don't any of you hear a sound?

KEEPER. The storm!
Merely the windows rattling in the storm.
Trucks going by to war. A war is on.

JONAH. That is no window. That's a showcase rattling.
That is your antiques rattling on a shelf.

JESSE BEL. You're doing it.

JONAH. I'm not. How could I be?

JESSE BEL. You're doing something to our minds.

JONAH. I'm not. –
Don't *you* feel something?

PAUL. Leave me out of this.

(He leans away in tolerant distaste.)

JONAH. And here come all your Great Books tumbling down!
You see the Lord God is a jealous God!
He wrote one book. Let there be no more written.
How are their volumes fallen!

KEEPER. Only one!

JONAH. Hold on there. Leave that open where it lies.
Be careful not to lose the place. Be careful.
Please let me have it.

JESSE BEL. Read us what it says.

JONAH. Look, will you look! God can't put words in my mouth.
My tongue's my own, as True Thomas used to say.

KEEPER. So you've been Bohning up on Thomism too.

JONAH. Someone else read it.

KEEPER. No, you read it to us.
And if it's prophecy, we'll see what happens.

JONAH. Nothing would happen. That's the thing of it.
God comes on me to doom a city for Him.
But oh, no, not for Jonah. I refuse
To be the bearer of an empty threat.
He may be God, but me, I'm only human:
I shrink from being publicly let down.

JESSE BEL. Is this the love of God you preached to me?

JONAH. There's not the least lack of the love of God
In what I say. Don't be so silly, woman.
His very weakness for mankind's endearing.

I love and fear Him. Yes, but I fear for Him.
I don't see how it can be to His interest,
This modern tendency I find in Him
To take the punishment out of all failure
To be strong, careful, thrifty, diligent,
Anything we once thought we had to be.

KEEPER. You know what lets us off from being careful?
The thing that did what you consider mischief,
That ushered in this modern lenience,
Was the discovery of fire insurance.
The future state is springing even now
From the discovery that loss from failure,
By being spread out over everybody,
Can be made negligible.

PAUL. What's your book?
What's this?

JONAH. Don't lose the place.

PAUL. Old Dana Lyle,
Who reconciled the Pentateuch with science.

JONAH. Where shall I start in? Where my eyes fell first?
It seems to be a chapter head in meter.

JESSE BEL. It's too big for him. Help him hold it up.

JONAH. Someone else read it.

KEEPER. No, you asked for it.

JESSE BEL. Come on, or we'll begin to be afraid.

JONAH. Well, but remember this is unofficial:
'The city's grotesque iron skeletons
Would knock their drunken penthouse heads together
And cake their concrete dirt off in the streets.'
Then further down it seems to start from where

The city is admittedly an evil:
'O city on insecure rock pedestal,
So knowing – and yet needing to be told
The thought that added cubits to your height
Would better have been taken to your depth.'
(*A whole shelf cascades down.*) Here come some more.
The folly crashes and the dust goes up.

(*When the dust settles it should be apparent
Something has altered in the outer door.*)

JESSE BEL. Mercy, for mercy's sake!

KEEPER. Bel wants some mercy. –
Kneel to your doctor. He dispenses mercy. –
You're working it, old man. Don't be discouraged.

JONAH. This isn't it. I haven't prophesied.
This is God at me in my skulking place,
Trying to flush me out. That's all it is.

KEEPER. It's nothing but the Lending Library.
All secondhand. Don't get excited, folks;
The one indecency's to make a fuss
About our own or anybody's end.

JONAH. It's nothing I brought on by words of mine.

KEEPER. You know, there may have been a small temblor.
If so, it will be in tomorrow's paper.

PAUL. Now if we've had enough of sacrilege,
We can go back to where we started from.
Let me repeat: I'm glad to hear you say
You can't trust God to be unmerciful.
What would you have God if not merciful?

JONAH. Just, I would have Him just before all else,
To see that the fair fight is really fair.

Then he could enter on the stricken field
After the fight's so definitely done
There can be no disputing who has won –
Then he could enter on the stricken field
As Red Cross Ambulance Commander-in-Chief
To ease the more extremely wounded out
And mend the others up to go again.

PAUL. I thought as much. You have it all arranged,
Only to see it shattered every day.
You should be an authority on Mercy.
That book of yours in the Old Testament
Is the first place in literature, I think,
Where Mercy is explicitly the subject.
I say you should be proud of having beaten
The Gospels to it. After doing Justice justice
Milton's pentameters go on to say,
But Mercy first and last shall brightest shine –
Not only last, but first, you will observe;
Which spoils your figure of the ambulance.

KEEPER. Paul only means you make too much of justice.
There's some such thing and no one will deny it –
Enough to bait the trap of the ideal
From which there can be no escape for us
But by our biting off our adolescence
And leaving it behind us in the trap.

JONAH. Listen, ye! It's the proletariat!
A revolution's coming down the street!
Lights out, I say, so's to escape attention.

(He snaps one bulb off. Paul snaps on another.)

JESSE BEL. You needn't shout like that, you wretched man.
There's nothing coming on us, is there, Paul?
We've had about enough of these sensations.

R.F.–12

It's a coincidence, but we were on
The subject of the workers' revolution
When you came in. We're revolutionists.
Or Keeper is a revolutionist.
Paul almost had poor Keeper in a corner
Where he would have to quit his politics
Or be a Christian. – Paul, I wish you'd say
That over. I shall have to retail it
To some of Keeper's friends that come in here,
A bunch of small-time revolutionaries. –
Paul makes it come out so they look like Christians.
How they'll like that. Paul said conservatives –
You say it, Paul.

PAUL. You mean about success,
And how by its own logic it concentrates
All wealth and power in too few hands?
The rich in seeing nothing but injustice
In their impoverishment by revolution
Are right. But 'twas intentional injustice.
It was their justice being mercy-crossed.
The revolution Keeper's bringing on
Is nothing but an outbreak of mass mercy,
Too long pent up in rigorous convention –
A holy impulse towards redistribution.
To set out to homogenize mankind
So that the cream could never rise again
Required someone who laughingly could play
With the idea of justice in the courts,
Could mock at riches in the right it claims
To count on justice to be merely just.
But we are talking over Jonah's head,
Or clear off what we know his interests are.
Still, not so far off, come to think of it.
There is some justice, even as Keeper says.

The thing that really counts, though, is the form
Of outrage – violence – that breaks across it.
The very sleep we sleep is an example.
So that because we're always starting fresh
The best minds are the best at premises.
And the most sacred thing of all's abruption.
And if you've got to see your justice crossed
(And you've got to), which will you prefer
To see it, evil-crossed or mercy-crossed?

KEEPER. We poets offer you another: star-crossed.
Of star-crossed, mercy-crossed, or evil-crossed
I choose the star-crossed as a star-crossed lover.

JONAH. I think my trouble's with the crisises
Where mercy-crossed to me seemed evil-crossed.

KEEPER. Good for you, Jonah. That's what I've been saying.
For instance, when to purify the Itzas
They took my love and threw her down a well.

JESSE BEL. If it is me in my last incarnation
He's thinking of, it wasn't down a well,
But in a butt of malmsey I was drowned.

JONAH. Why do you call yourself a star-crossed lover?

KEEPER. Not everything I say is said in scorn.
Some people want you not to understand them,
But I want you to understand me wrong.

JONAH. I noticed how he just now made you out
A revolutionary – which of course you can't be.

KEEPER. Or not at least the ordinary kind.
No revolution I brought on would aim
At anything but change of personnel.
The Andrew Jackson slogan of *Vae Victis*
Or 'Turn the rascals out' would do for me.

PAUL. Don't you be made feel small by all this posing.
Both of them caught it from Bel's favorite poet,
Who in his favorite pose as poet-thinker
(His was the doctrine of the Seven Poses)
Once charged the Nazarene with having brought
A darkness out of Asia that had crossed
Old Attic grace and Spartan discipline
With violence. The Greeks were hardly strangers
To the idea of violence. It flourished,
Persisting from old Chaos in their myth,
To embroil the very gods about their spheres
Of influence. It's been a commonplace
Ever since Alexander Greeced the world.
'Twere nothing new if that were all Christ brought
Christ came to introduce a break with logic
That made all other outrage seem as child's play:
The Mercy on the Sin against the Sermon.
Strange no one ever thought of it before Him.
'Twas lovely and its origin was love.

KEEPER. We know what's coming now.

PAUL. You say it, Keeper,
If you have learned your lesson. Don't be bashful.

KEEPER. Paul's constant theme. The Sermon on the Mount
Is just a frame-up to insure the failure
Of all of us, so all of us will be
Thrown prostrate at the Mercy Seat for Mercy.

JESSE BEL. Yes, Paul, you do say things like that sometimes.

PAUL. You all have read the Sermon on the Mount.
I ask you all to read it once again.

*(They put their hands together like a book
And hold it up nearsightedly to read.)*

KEEPER AND
JESSE BEL. We're reading it.

PAUL. Well, now you've got it read,
What do you make of it?

JESSE BEL. The same old nothing.

KEEPER. A beautiful impossibility.

PAUL. Keeper, I'm glad you think it beautiful.

KEEPER. An irresistible impossibility.
A lofty beauty no one can live up to,
Yet no one turn from trying to live up to.

PAUL. Yes, spoken so we can't live up to it,
Yet so we'll have to weep because we can't.
Mercy is only to the undeserving.
But such we all are made in the sight of God.

'Oh, what is a king here,
And what is a boor?
Here all starve together,
All dwarfed and poor.'

Here we all fail together, dwarfed and poor.
Failure is failure, but success is failure.
There is no better way of having it.
An end you can't by any means achieve,
And yet can't turn your back on or ignore,
That is the mystery you must accept. –
Do you accept it, Master Jonas Dove?

JONAH. What do you say to it, My Brother's Keeper?

KEEPER. I say I'd rather be lost in the woods
Than found in church.

JONAH. That doesn't help me much.

KEEPER. Our disagreement when we disagree, Paul,
Lies in our different approach to Christ,
Yours more through Rome, mine more through Palestine. –
But let's be serious about Paul's offer.
His irresistible impossibility,
His lofty beauty no one can live up to,
Yet no one turn away from or ignore –
I simply turn away from it.

PAUL. You Pagan!

KEEPER. Yes, call me Pagan, Paul, as if you meant it.
I won't deceive myself about success
By making failure out of equal value.
Any equality they may exhibit's
In making fools of people equally.

PAUL. But you – what is your answer, Jonas Dove?

JONAH. You ask if I see yonder shining gate,
And I reply I almost think I do,
Beyond this great door you have locked against me,
Beyond the storm, beyond the universe.

PAUL. Yes, Pilgrim now instead of runaway,
Your fugitive escape become a quest.

KEEPER. Don't let him make you see too bright a gate
Or you will come to with a foolish feeling.
When a great tide of argument sweeps in
My small fresh-water spring gets drowned of course.
But when the brine goes back, as go it must,
I can count on my source to spring again,
Not even brackish from its salt experience.
No true source can be poisoned.

JONAH. Then that's all.
You've finished. I'm dismissed. I want to run

Toward what you make me see beyond the world.
Unlock the door for me.

KEEPER. Not that way out.

JONAH. I'm all turned round.

PAUL. There is your way prepared.

JONAH. That's not my door.

KEEPER. No, that's another door.
Your exit door's become a cellar door.

(*The door here opens darkly of itself.*)

JONAH. You mean I'm being sent down in the cellar?

PAUL. You must make your descent like everyone.

KEEPER. Go if you're going.

JONAH. Who is sending me?
Whose cellar is it, yours or the apostle's?

KEEPER. It is the cellar to my store. – What ho, down there!
My dungeoneers, come fetch us. – No one answers.
There's not much we can do till Martin gets here. –
Don't let me scare you. I was only teasing.
It is the cellar to my store, but not my cellar.
Jesse has given Paul the rent of it
To base his campaign on to save the world.

JESSE BEL. Something's the matter, everyone admits.
On the off-chance it may be lack of faith,
I have contributed the empty cellar
To Paul to see what he can do with it
To bring faith back. I'm only languidly
Inclined to hope for much. Still what we need
Is something to believe in, don't we, Paul?

KEEPER. By something to believe in, Jesse means
Something to be fanatical about,
So as to justify the orthodox
In saving heretics by slaying them,
Not on the battlefield, but down in cellars.
That way's been tried too many times for me.
I'd like to see the world tried once without it.

JESSE BEL. The world seems crying out for a Messiah.

KEEPER. Haven't you heard the news? We already have one,
And of the Messianic race, Karl Marx.

JESSE BEL. Light, bring a light!

KEEPER. Awh, there's no lack of light, you –
A light that falls diffused over my shoulder
And is reflected from the printed page
And bed of world-flowers so as not to blind me.
If even the face of man's too bright a light
To look at long directly (like the sun),
Then how much more the face of truth must be.
We were not given eyes or intellect
For all the light at once the source of light –
For wisdom that can have no counterwisdom.
In our subscription to the sentiment
Of one God, we provide He shall be one
Who can be many Gods to many men,
His church on earth a Roman Pantheon;
Which is our greatest hope of rest from war.
Live and let live, believe and let believe.
'Twas said the lesser gods were only traits
Of the one awful God. Just so the saints
Are God's white light refracted into colors.

JESSE BEL. Let's change the subject, boys, I'm getting nervous.

KEEPER. Nervous is all the great things ever made you.
But to repeat and get it through your head:
We have all the belief that's good for us.
Too much all-fired belief and we'd be back
Down burning skeptics in the cellar furnace
Like Shadrach, Meshach, and Abednego.

JONAH. What's all this talk of slaying down in cellars –
So sinister? You spoke to someone down there.

KEEPER. My friends and stokers, Jeffers and O'Neill.
They fail me. Now I'm teasing you again.
There's no one down there getting tortured, save
A penitent perhaps, self-thrown on Mercy.

JONAH. I heard a deep groan – maybe out of him.
What's really down there?

PAUL. Just an oubliette,
Where you must lie in self-forgetfulness
On the wet flags before a crucifix
I have had painted on the cellar wall
By a religious Aztec Indian.

JONAH. Then it's not lethal – to get rid of me?
Have they been down?

PAUL. Not in the proper spirit.
These two are stubborn children, as you see.
Their case is not so simple. You are good.

JONAH. I am your convert. Tell me what I think.
My trouble has been with my sense of justice.
And you say justice doesn't really matter.

PAUL. Does it to you as greatly as it did?

JONAH. I own the need of it had somewhat faded
Even before I came in here tonight.

PAUL. Well then!

JONAH. And that's what I'm to meditate?

PAUL. Meditate nothing. Learn to contemplate.
Contemplate glory. There will be a light.
Contemplate Truth until it burns your eyes out.

JONAH. I don't see any staircase.

KEEPER. There are stairs.

PAUL. Some lingering objection holds you back.

JONAH. If what you say is true, if winning ranks
The same with God as losing, how explain
Our making all this effort mortals make?

KEEPER. Good for you, Jonah. That's what I've been saying.

JONAH. You'll tell me sometime. All you say has greatness.
Yet your friend here can't be quite disregarded.

KEEPER. I say we keep him till we wring some more
Naïveness about Justice out of him,
As once the Pharaoh did it out of Sekhti
By having him whipped every day afresh
For clamoring for justice at the gate,
Until the scribes had taken down a bookful
For distribution to his bureaucrats.

JONAH. I'm going now. But don't you push me off.

KEEPER. I was supporting you for fear you'd faint
From disillusionment. You've had to take it.

(Jonah steps on the threshold as the door
Slams in his face. The blow and the repulse
Crumple him on the floor. Keeper and Paul
Kneel by him. Bel stands up beside her chair
As if to come, but Keeper waves her off.)

JONAH. I think I may have got God wrong entirely.

KEEPER. All of us get each other pretty wrong.

JESSE BEL. Now we have done it, Paul. What did he say?

JONAH. I should have warned you, though, my sense of justice
Was about all there ever was to me.
When that fades I fade – every time I fade.
Mercy on me for having thought I knew.

JESSE BEL. What did he say? I can't hear what he says.

PAUL. Mercy on him for having asked for justice.

KEEPER. Die saying that, old-fashioned sapient,
You poor old sape, if I may coin the slang.
We like you, don't we, Paul? (*Paul takes his wrist.*)

JESSE BEL. (*Still standing off*) We've all grown fond of you.

PAUL. We've all grown fond of you. (*Paul says it louder, But Jonah gives no sign of having heard.*)

KEEPER. Who said, 'Too late, you cannot enter now'?

JESSE BEL. He was rejected for his reservations!

KEEPER. (*Still on his knees, he sits back on his heels.*)
But one thing more before the curtain falls. –
(*The curtain starts to fall.*) Please hold the curtain. –
All Paul means, and I wish the dead could hear me –
All you mean, Paul, I think —

JESSE BEL. Will you stand there
And let that tell you what you think, like that?

PAUL. Suffer a friend to try to word you better.

JESSE BEL. Oh, there's to be a funeral oration.
And we're an orator. Get up. Stand up

For what you think your doctor thinks, why don't you?
Don't wear your pants out preaching on your knees.
Save them to say your prayers on. – What's the matter?

KEEPER. (*He doesn't rise, but looks at her a moment.*)
Lady, at such a time, and in the Presence! –
I won't presume to tell Bel where to go.
But if this prophet's mantle fell on me
I should dare say she would be taken care of.
We send our wicked enemies to Hell,
Our wicked friends we send to Purgatory.
But Bel gets some things right – and she was right –

JESSE BEL. (*She startles at the sudden note of kindness.*)
I *am* right, then?

KEEPER. – In glorifying courage.
Courage is of the heart by derivation,
And great it is. But fear is of the soul.
And I'm afraid. (*The bulb lights sicken down.*
The cellar door swings wide and slams again.)

PAUL. The fear that you're afraid with is the fear
Of God's decision lastly on your deeds.
That is the Fear of God whereof 'tis written.

KEEPER. But not the fear of punishment for sin
(I have to sin to prove it isn't that).
I'm no more governed by the fear of Hell
Than by the fear of the asylum, jail, or poorhouse,
The basic three the state is founded on.
But I'm too much afraid of God to claim
I have been fighting on the angels' side.
That is for Him and not for me to say.
For me to say it would be irreligious.
(Sometimes I think you are too sure you have been.)
And I can see that the uncertainty

In which we act is a severity,
A cruelty, amounting to injustice
That nothing but God's mercy can assuage.
I can see that, if that is what you mean.
Give me a hand up, if we are agreed.

PAUL. Yes, there you have it at the root of things.
We have to stay afraid deep in our souls
Our sacrifice – the best we have to offer,
And not our worst nor second best, our best,
Our very best, our lives laid down like Jonah's,
Our lives laid down in war and peace – may not
Be found acceptable in Heaven's sight.
And that they may be is the only prayer
Worth praying. May my sacrifice
Be found acceptable in Heaven's sight.

KEEPER. Let the lost millions pray it in the dark!
My failure is no different from Jonah's.
We both have lacked the courage in the heart
To overcome the fear within the soul
And go ahead to any accomplishment.
Courage is what it takes and takes the more of
Because the deeper fear is so eternal.
And if I say we lift him from the floor
And lay him where you ordered him to lie
Before the cross, it is from fellow-feeling,
As if I asked for one more chance myself
To learn to say (*He moves to Jonah's feet*)
Nothing can make injustice just but mercy.

Curtain

INDEX OF FIRST LINES

INDEX OF TITLES